HOW TO CREATE A BUSINESS THAT
THRIVES
IN YOUR ABSENCE

...The Exciting Story Of An Ambitious Indian Hunter

DR. ABIB OLAMITOYE

How To Create A Business That Thrives In Your Absence
Copyright © 2010 By Abib Olamitoye

All rights reserved. No portion of this book may be reproduced, stored in a retrieval system, or transmitted in any form or by any means - electronic, mechanical, photocopy, scanning, or other - except for brief quotation in critical reviews or articles, without the prior written permission of the publisher.

The entire story in this book is made up. All the characters are fictitious and the essence does not attempt to harm the image or reputation of any individual or organizations.

Published in Nigeria by
100/10 Publications
E-mail: villageboy2009@ymail.com or olamitoye@aol.com
Tel: +234(0)8030655903

ISBN 978-978-903-957-9

Printed in the Federal Republic of Nigeria

HOW TO CREATE A BUSINESS THAT THRIVES IN YOUR ABSENCE

...The Exciting Story Of An Ambitious Indian Hunter

CONTENTS

DEDICATION vi
ACKNOWLEDGMENT ix
FOREWORD xi
ENCOURAGING TESTIMONIES
Testimony 1 xiii
Testimony 2 xiv
Testimony 3 xv
Testimony 4 xvi
Testimony 5 xviii
Testimony 6 xix
Testimony 7 xxi
Testimony 8 xxi
Testimony 9 xxiii
Testimony 10 xxiii
Testimony 11 xxiv
Testimony 12 xxiv
Testimony 13 xx
Testimony 14 xxvii

INTRODUCTION
The Ambitious Indian Hunter 1

CHAPTER ONE
A Life Of Serenity; Peace 15

CHAPTER TWO
How To Make People Do What You Want   27

CHAPTER THREE
The Fire Of Desire   51

CHAPTER FOUR
Creating An Enduring Business System   65

CHAPTER FIVE
Great Ways To Hire Great People   79

CHAPTER SIX
The Amazing Power of Delegation   105

CHAPTER SEVEN
Firing Incompetent People   127

CHAPTER EIGHT
Conclusion   139

DEDICATION

This work is dedicated in loving memory of my late father and affectionate friend, Yaya Olamitoye, and to the Glory of God.

ACKNOWLEDGMENT

I thank God for enabling this work. I thank my wife, Olubunmi Gbenuade, my children Oluwaseun and Opeyemi for their love, support and encouragement.

I deeply appreciate the phenomenal contributions of my great mentors whose breakthrough ideas and revolutionary products have helped to shape the character and substance of this book. In particular, I stay indebted to Dr. Joe Vitale, Brian Tracy and Dr. Wayne W. Dyer.

I thank all the amazing staff of i-universe (U.S.A) and New York Publices (U.S.A) for their super efforts during the publication of 'the greatest & strangest MONEY MAKING SECRETS.'

I thank my friend, Dr. Oluleke Badmos of Toronto East General Hospital, Canada, for being a priceless and selfless agent with the publishers.

I thank 'Tokunbo DesMennu who has become an irreplaceable companion. I am grateful to my secretary, Adedayo Temitope, for her diligence and endurance during the setting and correcting of the drafts for this book. My editor, Mrs. Ayo-Lawal Gbenoba of the African Newspapers of Nigeria (AAN) Plc has been as fantastic as ever. I thank the Publisher of AAN Plc. Resolution Oluwole Awolowo and all the wonderful staff and management of the Nigeria Tribune Newspapers for their love and support.

I stay grateful to Dr. BGK Ajayi for writing such an inspiring forward, and for the monumental achievement of bringing entrepreneural training to the university community. I thank Professor Olusegun Akinyinka, the Provost of the College of Medicine, University of Ibadan, for his love and encouragement. I sincerely appreciate the thoughtfulness of the immediate past Provost, Professor Omigbodun, for endorsing the use of the College Auditorium for the monthly seminars.

I acknowledge the incredible contributions of the following members of the 100/10 Academy: Dr. Tayo Apampa of Korede Hospital; Mr. Jayeola Taiwo of the Continental Suites; Mr. & Mrs. Rilwan Olamitoye, Mrs. Bunmi Apampa, Dr. Agbamu Charles Sagua, Mr. Babatunde Olaniyi, Sir Adams Momoh, Mr. & Mrs. Kunle Oluwole and all the ambassadors and associate members of the academy.

I thank all contributors to this work, especially the powerful writings of all those who took the time to share their happy testimonies.

Finally, I thank you, my dear friend and co-passenger on this exciting trip for investing your time and money.

I love you all.

Abib Olamitoye

FOREWORD

There are three parts to this book. The first is the real life story of the author himself. The second is the fable of the hunter and the parrot. The third is the message which the author wants to convey on how to manage your business in your absence.

A man cannot talk passionately and convincingly about what he doesn't believe in. As much as he may try, there will be noticeable gaps in delivery, which will give him away. Dr. Abib Olamitoye is quiet and unassuming. Those who know him will accept that this book is a real life story. He lives by example; he practises in detail what he has described in this book.

Just like there is no exaggeration in Abib's life, there is no embellishment in this book. Even though, Abib's primary calling is Medicine, he has been able to remove the lid of professional jingoism in the complicated and entirely different field of Business to demonstrate that compartmentalisation in knowledge is artificial.

Whether it is Medicine, Engineering, Sociology, Business or any discipline whatever, there is an intricate link between them all – it's all about survival on this planet.

When Abib requested that I should read the manuscript and write the foreword, he also gave me a generous time limit to complete the assignment. I spent almost double the time. Why? You cannot read this book in a hurry. There is an interesting story of the hunter and the parrot, which is used as a medium to deliver the message about managing a business. It is a gripping story which held me spellbound. The language is simple and precise. It can be understood by all and sundry. Therein lies the danger and the danger is real! One can easily get lost in the story and forget about the message.

Every sentence conveys a powerful message. So I had to read, pause and reflect before moving on. Thus, the reader must keep the title of the book in mind in order to avoid getting lost in the interesting and compelling story and missing the beautiful message.

Abib is a fantastic writer and teacher. This book is so simply written that all grades of people can read and understand. He has removed the barrier between business and everyday living. One is made to see "that the business of managing or governance is essentially the same, whether it is organising a home, a kitchen, an hotel, a hospital or a nation."

This book is a must read for all who aspire to leadership, for all those who aspire to better life - who want the good things of life - who aspire to wealth. There is so much to learn in the story of the hunter and the parrot and I have gained tremendously. It is a great honour and privilege to write this foreword. Those who fail to follow the concept of managing a business as espoused by the parrot will not only have difficulty keeping it, they will become greedy, intolerant and selfish. Sadly, they are bound to lose all.

DR. BENEDICTUS 'GBOYEGA 'KUNLE AJAYI
MB.BS.,(Ibadan) MHS. (Johns Hopkins), FMCOph.,FWACS
President of Ibadan College of Medicine Alumni Association (Worldwide)
2007 Winner of the Labib Gold Medal Award for Ophthalmology, by the Middle East African Council of Ophthalmology (MEACO).
Winner of the G.OH. Naumann Award for Leadership in Global Eye Care from the International Council of Ophthalmology presented at the World Congress of Ophthalmology in, Hong Kong in June 2008. He is a Honorary Visiting Consultant to the U.C.H., Ibadan and Group Medical Director, Catholic Eye Hospitals. He earns a living working as a consultant ophthalmologist at Ojulowo Eye Clinic, Mokola, Ibadan

ENCOURAGING TESTIMONIES

TESTIMONY 1

I have been running a private hospital in Abeokuta, Nigeria, for the past 30 years. It has been very frustrating and energy-sapping, so much so that I felt like a prisoner of the hospital. Then I heard of a man who was running three hospitals in Nigeria but was living in England. That man is Dr. Abib Olamitoye. I listened to him, read his books and attended his seminars conducted at the 100/10 Academy in Abeokuta and Ibadan, Nigeria.

Since then, using the principles he taught, I have not only expanded my present hospital, I have started a second one where I do not work! I am not only fulfilled and living the lifestyle I love, I am brimming with ideas and bursting with energy.

DR. TAYO APAMPA
Korede Hospitals
17, Onikolobo Road, Ibara
26, Ogunsanya Street, Kugba
Abeokuta, Ogun State, Nigeria

TESTIMONY 2

Twelve years ago, when I completed my postgraduate fellowship training as a Family Physician, I wanted to go into private medical practice. I believed I had the knowledge and skills for a successful practice. But looking at those who had started before me, I soon got discouraged from pursuing the idea. Most of the people in private practice that I saw were always under stress; they grew grey hair very early, they were not able to join social and professional meetings and they were not able to develop themselves through further training. I also noticed that many of them could not go for holidays for years and as they age, the practice ages with them and the practice often dies when they are incapacitated or dead.

Then, three years ago, I met Dr Abib Olamitoye through Dr Apampa and started learning the principles of entrepreneurship, which were never taught in medical schools and postgraduate colleges.

I soon realized that the knowledge and skills required to run a successful medical business are different from the skills required to be a good doctor.

Within a year of learning from Dr. Olamitoye, I was able to start my practice on a good footing. The practice now runs largely without my presence and I am beginning to experience some level of time freedom and financial comfort.

More importantly, I am able to attend courses and workshops for personal development. I am confident that with the principles taught by Dr. Olamitoye, I will soon be able to completely delegate my practice and move on to replicate the practice in many other locations.

Dr. Olamitoye's teachings are based on time-tested, reliable, universally applicable principles backed by years of personal practical experience. His teachings are comprehensive, embracing, not only business success, but also principles for a successful life. It is always a wonderful experience to listen to him and learn from his wealth of experience.

If it's about business and life success, Dr Olamitoye has been 'there' and he is passionate about helping others get there.

DR. S.O. MALOMO
Head of Department, Federal Medical Centre, Abeokuta.
Coordinator, National Health Insurance Scheme,
Federal Medical Centre, Abeokuta.
Proprietor/Medical Director, Peace of God Medical Centre, Oke-Ilewo, Abeokuta

TESTIMONY 3

Once in a while, someone comes along who can lead, help and mentor others to their chosen life goals. Dr Abib Olamitoye is one. I have read many books, his book *'The Greatest and Strangest Money Making Secrets,'* is one of the few that combines planes of human existence (i.e. Mental, Physical, & Spiritual) as requisite to wealth creation and happiness, using the ingredients of Honesty, Hard work, Humility, Patience, Perseverance and Charity. No wonder, these are the basic values of 100/10 Academy of which he is the Founder. Reading his book and attending a meeting of the Academy made me resolve to join the Academy of which I am now a proud Ambassador.

Since I so resolved, it has tremendously navigated me in my chosen vocation/undertakings, as an Entrepreneur, of which, for a period, I was groping in the dark.

His latest book: 'HOW TO CREATE A BUSINESS THAT THRIVES IN YOUR ABSENCE', is not only an appropriate follow-up to *'The Greatest and Strangest Money-making Secrets'* but a compendium of his monthly mentoring lectures in the 100/10 Academy.

It has helped me to differentiate between being a Self-Employed Businessman, which I was, and being a Business Owner (Entrepreneur), which I am now.

The two books, in my humble opinion, are a must read and library stock for Entrepreneurs.

More grease, or should I say, dispensing, to Dr Abib Olamitoye, the little village boy, now a legend.

EVANGELIST M.A.O. OYENEYE Esq. JP

TESTIMONY 4

In fact, my coming in contact with Dr. Abib Olamitoye, through the 100/10 Academy, Abeokuta, via Dr. Tayo Apampa, has given my entire life a new meaning. The teachings of the 100/10 Academy monthly seminar transformed me, took me away from the world of impossibility and unveiled the VAST WORLD OF POSSIBILITIES AND GREAT OPPORTUNITIES to me! It is very rare to find someone who genuinely loves to show other people the way to success and at the same time, being highly enthusiastic to guide and motivate you, while sharing with you his very personal experiences and being unreserved about it!

His best selling book, 'THE GREATEST AND STRANGEST MONEY MAKING SECRETS' which is a product of the 100/10

Academy, really challenged, motivated and assured me that greatness in life is the function of your mind set, which lies in GOAL SETTING (whether consciously or unconsciously set goals). The inaugural meeting of the 100/10, Abeokuta, which was held on the 1st of February, 2007, was a turning point in my life, because it gave me a new direction entirely! I mean THE GOAL SETTING TOUR! That was my first time of being enthusiastic and determined about setting a reasonable, realistic and worthwhile goal in my life.

This GOAL SETTING TOUR has helped me dare to join the camp of millionaires with my net worth of less than 15% of 1 Million in year 2007. It is really a rare privilege to be a member of this Academy. Diverse lectures have been delivered by Dr. Abib Olamitoye, covering all aspects of life: PARETO PRINCIPLE, KAIZEN, HIRING THE RIGHT PERSON, CREATING A BUSINESS THAT RUNS SUCCESSFULLY IN YOUR ABSENCE, HEALTHY LIVING, STRESS MANAGEMENT and many more.

Right now, the story of my life has changed, from a petty trader in 2007 to a Director of my own duly registered limited liability company in the name of JELIZ INTEGRATED SERVICES LIMITED, with the 3M FOOD CENTER as a subsidiary. The 3M FOOD CENTRE is an experimental project of the 100/10 Academy seminars, with 2 branches in Abeokuta, the capital of Ogun State, within 14 months!

Long live Dr. Tayo Apampa! Long live 100/10 Academy!! Long live Dr. Abib Olamitoye!!!

LIZZY ADEBOYEJO.

TESTIMONY 5

Dr Abib Olamitoye actually saved my professional and personal lives after attending the 100/10 Academy.

I set up my private hospital (Lafia Hospital) in October 1991, in Ibadan, Nigeria and opened up a branch 6 years later, in 1997. Since then, it has always been work 24/7, all the way. I was always glued to my practice, having no time for holidays and even little time for my family. I have always believed in having to do it myself until my first seminar with the 100/10 Academy in June 2004. This proved to be the turn-key revolution in my life. My 1st seminar was on goal setting, which was mind blowing and fascinating. This was followed by series of others; People Skills, Hiring and Dehiring, Delegation, Principle Of Detachment etc.

The seminar on the Principle Of Detachment actually gave me the freedom I so much cherished: the freedom I thought impossible as a business owner. What I love most is the KISS technique (keep it short and simple) adopted by Dr Abib Olamitoye. I was trained step by step on the procedure in operating a business system; a system that will work in my absence.

Using the method for 4 years, I finally got a breakthrough in January, 2008 when I fully detached from active practice from the hospital where I have been tied down for 17 years. It is a feat I never thought possible, having freedom to go on holidays with my family. It is a dream come true that I can work on my business rather than in it. That was the momentum needed for me to think, being free to set up another business, the health insurance organization called NonSuch Medicare Limited, of which I am the MD/CEO.

I intend to reciprocate this same proven system in my new company. All the lectures received from the seminars I have attended have been translated into his current book 'HOW TO CREATE A BUSINESS THAT THRIVES IN YOUR ABSENCE.'

The concepts in this book are real and proven and can be implemented from the very next day. It is a ticket to a better future for you. It is a must read. Try the proven techniques and principles and you bet that your life will never be the same again.

DR DIPO SULE
MD/CEO NONSUCH HMO
CHAIRMAN, LAFIA GROUP OF HOSPITALS

TESTIMONY 6
Dear Dr. Abib,

Thank your very much for all I have gained since joining the 100/10 Academy in September 2009.

I have attended all lectures, and listened to all the CD/MP3, read your books: 'The Greatest And Strangest Money Making Secrets' and 'How To Create A Business That Thrives In Your Absence' - the exciting story of an ambitious Indian hunter. Before now I had set up a clinic since 1991, May 1st and by 1997 May, there was no doubt it was a failed business!!! It was due to lack of business knowledge!!!! Since September 1st 2009 I have set up another clinic/hospital and at the end of a year it is a success story so far due largely to the input from my attending 100/10 Academy and God! The bedrock of the Academy to me is YOU, Dr. Abib Olatimoye and all members' inputs and the contents of the Academy teachings - GOAL SETTING IN WRITING,

DETACHMENT (TO DIE-WHILE-STILL-LIVING), DELEGATING, PEOPLE SKILLS, HIRING AND DEHIRING (FIRING) OF STAFF, NEGOTIATION SKILLS, SELLING WELL AND ADVERTISING, MEETINGS, EXECUTIVE HEALTH ISSUES, PERSEVERANCE, LAWS OF MONEY, KAIZEN, PARETO PRINCIPLE, EXECUTIVE TIME MANAGEMENT, CREATING AN ENDURING BUSINESS STRUCTURE, ETC. And most importantly, reading widely for continuous personal and profession development.

THE DAY YOU DO NOT READ YOU ARE DEAD!!!! Once more let me thank you Dr. Abib Olatimoye and the 100 / 10 Academy team as an example of good management team for me and my business team and FOR TEACHING ME THINGS I WAS NOT TAUGHT IN ALL THE YEARS OF MY FORMAL SCHOOLING!!! THANK YOU! THANK YOU!! AND THANK YOU!!!

AGBAMU CHARLES SAGUA, (M.B.B.S(IB), F.R.C.S.ED., F.W.A.C.S.W.Afr.)
Consultant Primary Care / Rural Surgeon,
Division of Primary Care / Rural Surgery, Surgery Department,
University College Hospital, Ibadan and General Hospital, Igbo-ora,
P.O. Box 345, Igbo-Ora, Oyo State, Nigeria.
Tel:+2348073915501, +2347083094224

TESTIMONY 7

This book is invaluable in helping entrepreneurs who are established but more so those starting out afresh. It helps them to take that leap of confidence and embark upon definite steps to help promote business establishments for long term growth. Great success is not limited to certain people but available to all, achieved by hard work and diligence. This is what the author describes in this book.

The format, though initially intriguing, eventually flows into a rich and informative guide which provides a well thought out plan that lays bare the author's deepest thoughts and keenness to share his ideas. The book provides a very useful insight and guide into leading a life of inner peace and can be applied on both a personal level, in day-to-day interactions with family and friends as well as on a professional level with business or work colleagues and acquaintances alike.

I recommend the book to all.

DR. DUPE JIBODU
York, U.K.

TESTIMONY 8

The book serves as a living spring to me now that I have read it and can testify that it has further given me the zeal and courage to remain on course as the author - Dr. Abib, had played the role of the rich Yakubu to me in the book, on a personal note, for several years, on how to ' die- while- alive ' but I did not yield to him because of the fear of the unknown and not knowing how to delegate in full terms. This made me to cage myself for nineteen years doing so many of the activities on my own without any vacation. After his mentoring sessions on how to hire the ideal personnel and how to delegate, we did the recruitment through his hospital.

Behold, he stretched me further by helping to put systems on ground for checks and balances with a standard organogram, all as spelt out in this book. A few months later I was able to go on vacation to Singapore in 2007, to India for a conference in 2009 and to Cancun,-Mexico and California in 2010 for vacation/conference. With the applications of all the teachings given by the rich Yakubu in this book to the hunter and the zoo manager from Dehli in India, I can humbly and boldly say that I have gained some freedom to the level that my ventures - the hospital, the pharmaceutical outfit and the ultrasonography centre are thriving well even in my absence.

I therefore recommend this book as a must-read for whoever wants to move up the rungs on the ladder to great achievements in life.

SIR (DR.) F.F. ADAMS-MOMOH.
Chairman, Momoh Holdings Ltd.,
Oyo, Oyo State, Nigeria.

TESTIMONY 9

This book written by my friend, Dr. Abib Olamitoye is indeed a prophetic voice to the business world. This book will erupt a success revolution in the world. It is an epitome of divine wisdom to sweat less exploits.

PASTOR VICTOR AJISAFE,
President and Founder, Christ Revival Evangelistic Ministries and the Senior Pastor of the thriving fastest growing church in Sierra Leone, West Africa (Sanctuary Praise Church).

TESTIMONY 10

I needed to relocate abroad for a couple of years and could not fathom how the existing family business would continue to exist without me 'the mother hen'

After 90 minutes consultation session with Dr. Olamitoye, I came out in smiles, exited and empowered. Fresh adrenalin flowed as I now have a workable blueprint. One can indeed run any business autopilot, regardless of the size or location. I now use the same strategy to coach small business owners on how to retire young. Dr. Olamitoye is retired and young by practicing what he teaches.

This book is loaded, so, be prepared to be empowered.

BIBI BUNMI APAMPA
www.mybusinesscoach.biz
London, United Kingdom.

TESTIMONY 11

Since I have been reading books on wealth creation, I have finally come across the one book I can read and get all the ingredients needed to become financially independent.

Creativity, imagination and great artistry in presentation makes the book 'HOW TO CREATE A BUSINESS THAT THRIVES IN YOUR ABSENCE' a fantastic classic. Dr. Abib Olamitoye has proved it beyond any reasonable doubt that it is not what you do that matters in the game of money making, but how you do it; the process are the same, be it of Parrots Colony, Delhi Zoo, restaurant, banking or even the health sector. Thank you for being a deliverance minister in the ministry of money.

How to create a business that thrives in your absence is a must read for anyone that desires wealth.

BABATUNDE OLANIYI (TIOCOMMON)
Veteran Radio Broadcaster

TESTIMONY 12

TREMENDOUS REVOLUTION THAT STORMED MY FAMILY IN 100/10 ACADEMY

The teaching of Pareto principle made a lot of impact on me early year 2008 when I enlisted as a member. I now keep 20% of friends that give me 80% of fulfilment. I also now do 20% of tasks that produce 80% of fantastic results.

My communication skill verbally and on paper improved greatly in the year 2009 when emphasis was laid on the topic. I now treasure relationships better that quick financial gains. As an author, I learnt to regularly use 'magic sentences' in my publications towards the end of the year 2009. My perception of quality was greatly enlightened in the year 2010 as topics focused round it. I noticed a greater social and intellectual development more than ever in me as a result of this.

Though I don't have chains of hospitals and business outlets like Dr. Abib and Dr. Apampa, I am now blessed with multiple sources of income that I believe will make me join and continue to *'think like'* the happy team of billionaires all over the world in a few years time.

Dr. Olamitoye, a celebrity today and his amiable team, thank you for your humility and patience with all members. My family including my children who are also member of 100/10 academy say well done.

PHARM. OLUWAGBENGA ODUNFA
Tel: +234(0)8037126511
E mail: godunfa@yahoo.com

TESTIMONY 13

I had the opportunity of reviewing a complimentary copy of the book before the final print for which I am grateful.

I would like to once again commend Dr. Abib Olamitoye for a great Effort ! Well done. This book is completely packed right from the very first chapter to the last. On practical and well tested tips on how to create a business that thrives in your absence.

The author is a qualified medical practitioner & consultant in Healthcare Management. He is also an investor, writer, motivational speaker, mentor, Multimillionaire and founder of the 100/10 Academy. He has drawn from his rich wealth of practical experience in Business and Management spanning over 25 years to produce this piece of work in addition to the other resources cited in the book.

The style of writing I must admit is clearly different from that used in his first book 'The Greatest and Strangest money making secrets.' The Context here is set within a hypothetical Animal Kingdom to reflect the structure of Society at large and organizational structure and hierarchy of a small to medium scale business but no doubt larger organizations will also benefit from it.

Initially the reader may wonder what has a Zoological garden or forest or that indeed what has animal kingdom got to do with creating a business. But the book is 'loaded' and is high voltage and I recommend it to the reader.

Well done Abib!

DR. J OLUBOKUN
MD/CEO PENUEL UK Ltd
London, October 2010.

Consultant Psychiatrist & Lead Clinician
Highly Specialist Tier for Adolescent In-Patient Unit Poplar Unit,
Rochford Hospital, South Essex University Partnership NHS Trust
Essex, United Kingdom.
Special Advisor to the Consul of Niger Republic to Great Britain
Chairman/CEO, PENUEL MINING CO. LIMITED
Aggregates and Quality Granite
FCT, Abuja, Nigeria

TESTIMONY 14

If I am to write about the many benefits I have derived from 100/10 Academy, I would need an entire book to do so. For this reason, I would limit myself to saying that the 100/10 Academy has greatly influenced my spiritual, domestic and financial life.

It has helped me to get rid of the "employee mentality" which has been replaced by the "Entrepreneurial mentality".

Dr. Abib Olamitoye, through 100/10 Academy has taught me how to get whatever I want in Life, no matter how outrageous it may appear at first, by taking tested and trusted steps as shared monthly by Dr Abib Olamitoye.

I have been putting the teachings of the seminar to test and it has been working like magic every time!

GRACE OLUWOLE
Columnist (Sun Newspaper, Nigeria)
October 2010

INTRODUCTION

The Ambitious Indian Hunter

Once upon a time, many years ago, there was an Indian hunter who loved the animals and birds of Africa. He paid yearly visits to the woods, the thick forests of Africa and went away with prized animals and rare birds, which he displayed in his mighty zoo in New Delhi, India.

During one of his visits, he came across a colony of strange and precious parrots with colourful feathers and unique features. He stood in awe for hours as he watched these delightful birds sang and flew joyously from twig to twig atop a great Mahogany tree.

There was something unusual about these birds, he thought. Suddenly, strange ideas began to form in his head. If this display could impress him this much, it would probably impress people in their millions.

"This could carry some commercial value," he thought.

How could he make the most of this? Could this fill the need for entertainment? he questioned. It would be absurd to bring people from India to watch these birds and then get

Introduction

them to pay him. The land and the tree did not belong to him. How then could he take advantage of this? How could he take these birds to India so that people would derive entertainment and as a result, he would become rich?

Suppose he could lay his fingers on some of these birds, he would build a huge cage over a big tree in his zoo and then put them in it. How about paying a yearly pilgrimage to this Mahogany tree to catch birds after birds, and who knows, he could relocate the entire colony to his zoo in India.

Soon, this idea began to consume him. Nothing could possibly be more fascinating than to sit and watch these birds sing and dance and fly in a tree cage in his zoo. The entire people of Asia would queue to get their zoo tickets. 'How glorious would this turn out to be?' he thought. 'How prosperous and famous would he become?' Extremely overwhelming emotions can intoxicate the best hearts, as wine the strongest heads. In a feat of excitement, he began to dance and sing some popular Hindi songs to celebrate his happy expectation of the dawn of prosperity. His days of glory were suddenly within a touching distance. He delved triumphantly into hilarious love songs from great Hindi films.

Soon, a few of the parrots began to chorus his songs. He was unaware at first but became pleasantly surprised as the entire colony of these birds began to sing ancient Hindi

Introduction

songs, the classic songs sung during great ceremonies in New Delhi and other great cities and villages across India.

The hunter got even more overwhelmed. He had never witnessed anything this exciting. This was the nicest thing that would happen in the ten years of his annual pilgrimage to this tropical rainforest, this was the strangest and most pleasant occurrence of his existence.

This development made him sink deeper into his dream to take these parrots back to his zoo. Indians would desire to rent a collection of them during birthday and marriage ceremonies. The thought of producing audio CDs and DVDs of these birds, their sales in major retail shops, plus the pleasure of counting rupees in millions, could be very sweet and sensational.

'How much would he charge the great Indian actors and actresses were they to need his birds to brighten the scenes in their films?' he thought ambitiously. His birds and zoo would feature prominently on the pages of newspapers. Radio channels and television programmes would air stories and documentaries of his zoo. He would become an instant celebrity, an instant billionaire.

The hunter was too engrossed in thought to notice as the sun descended quietly behind the great trees of this tropical rainforest, and neither was he aware that the birds had since stopped singing and had all kept quiet in their peaceful nests. He stopped further singing and dancing.

Introduction

He had to return to his tent that night very tired, but in a high spirit and with great excitement as to the limitless opportunities and sumptuous possibilities beckoning him.

The song and jubilation within the ranks of these glorious parrots woke him up at dawn. This day, he was going to do something decisive about his dream. He would have to make his dream of fame and prosperity come true.

He spent the entire morning planning, devising and applying several methods and strategies to catch one or two of these delightful birds. He wanted them alive. A dead parrot would fetch him nothing more than a decent barbecue, at best. This would certainly not make him rich nor make him famous, he thought.

To get a live bird, however, became a very challenging exercise. He never anticipated this degree of difficulty. He set traps, threw nets, laid ambush and conjured ingenious ideas, powerful techniques and petty tricks. All to no avail.

He would probably need the combination of two or three long ladders to reach the lowest branch of the tree. The thought of falling from one of these ladders and then dying slowly in this lonely forest made the idea of ladder construction seem frightening and unsafe. No law abiding and rational man would choose to die by hanging in this forest, with a nasty picture of a rope and some clumsy ladder. He shook his head as he dismissed the ladder

Introduction

option. But, there must be a way. He went on thinking.

He toyed briefly with the notion of climbing the tree itself. The trunk was too mighty and the bark was very slippery. He then began to modify the character of his thoughts. How could he get hold of some of the eggs? He could hatch them, and who knows, he could come up with a new generation of beautiful parrots. This would take time, he thought. Besides, it might require the services of a mother parrot to do the hatching. Smashing the eggs open might prove senseless and unrewarding.

Suddenly, he heard a loud noise on the dry leaves underneath the Mahogany tree a few meters away from where he stood; to have a look, he went closer and, behold, a big parrot was lying helplessly on its back. He could not believe his eyes. He went closer and made a reflex dive in the direction of the bird, caught it and then struggled to his feet. He held on to the legs and wings, and then took a thorough look. Was it sick or dead? It seemed to be breathing and moving. He quickly kept it in a cage he had constructed. Could this be a source of hope?

The labour had been intensive and the hunter at this time had become very exhausted and homesick. He would have to take the bird to India and care for it. This is a bird in hand, he thought, which could be a lot better than the rest on the tree. He packed his bags and headed home.

Introduction

Happily, the bird had become active and healthy long before his arrival in New Delhi.

He constructed a larger and more beautiful cage for his new pet. He was to learn much later that his parrot had the capacity to sing as much as the capacity to speak. It could speak any language.

Soon, they became great friends. They talked and shared experiences on many issues. The hunter cared for it and procured the finest grain and the purest water to keep the bird healthy and happy.

One year later, the hunter was to go back to Africa. He had come up with fresh ideas on how to bring more parrots to India. This time, he was not going to use any trick or bait. He had prepared a well articulated speech that could persuade some of these birds to follow him. He would take advantage of his new awareness that they could understand his language.

He was very excited. All he had to do to keep his dream of prosperity alive would be to influence two or three dozens of birds to follow him each year. His spirit rose higher. He told his friend, the parrot, that he would be going back to the African forest and that he would reach its friends and relatives. He asked the parrot if there was any special message it would want him to convey to the other birds.

The parrot thanked him and wished him well on his trip.

Introduction

The other parrots should be told how much it enjoyed its cage in India; the great weather, the loving people, the rare seeds and the caring hunter. They should also be told how much he missed them, his loving family and the great king.

The hunter delivered the message upon arrival. "My parrot in its model cage back home in India love you dearly and miss you greatly," he concluded proudly. As soon as he mentioned the last word, one of the birds on the tree suddenly chanted a loud panicky noise, became stiff, fell from the branch and landed heavily on the dry leaves at the bottom of the Mahogany tree, and died.

The hunter, who had not anticipated this sort of development, became disturbed. The sad scene moved him beyond measure. There was a great silence in the woods. He must have caused a great harm in the colony, the hunter thought. He felt the dead bird had missed its friend so dearly that it developed intense pain, which resulted in instant death.

If this was the degree of damage the idea of taking many birds away would unleash; if his dream would kill, if his plans and ambition would elicit further calamity within this kingdom; it would be prudent to surrender the plan in its entirety. His elaborate speech would persuade no bird, under this circumstance, anyway. Delivering such a speech would only serve to make him seem cruel and

Introduction

inconsiderate. No bird would listen. He felt very ashamed, apologetic and guilty. He went ahead to express sympathy and promised the birds to relate the sad news to his friend, the parrot, on his arrival. His lofty idea of instant prosperity and fame suddenly, and sadly, began to take wings.

The hunter left the birds on a sad note and went to the other parts of the forest where he caught several animals and returned to India. He could hardly wait to get a complete explanation of the entire misery.

The hunter told his parrot upon arrival of the astonishing attitude of one of its relatives after he had delivered the message. "It went into a trance, made a loud noise, became stiff, fell off the branch, landed heavily and died," he concluded.

As soon as the parrot in the cage heard this, it too made a similar noise, became stiff, fell on the floor of the cage with its legs to the ceiling and died. The hunter was confused and furious, and in desperation, he opened the cage, held the stiff legs of the dead parrot and threw the carcass into the garden. "Nonsense," he uttered.

As soon as the bird landed in the garden, the stiff legs came alive again and the bird flew to the branch of a tree in the garden. The hunter felt very disappointed, betrayed and then he piled relentless accusation on the resurrected bird.

"I love you with all my heart!" he lamented profusely. "I

Introduction

cared for you with all my cash; I fed you the rarest grains and the purest water. This shameless trick, this dubious escape plan is all I get for my troubles. Why do this to me?," the hunter demanded.

"My recent death was real. It was neither dubious nor was it calculated to hurt you," the parrot began his defence. "I love you. I admire you. I appreciate your care and treasure your friendship. I would do no such thing designed to bite the finger that feeds me," he continued.

"The message you brought from my relatives in Africa was coded. Human beings and parrots have two essential attributes in common; the capacity to speak any language and the capacity to 'die-while-alive.'

"God in His infinite love and wisdom granted these two attributes for the benefit of parrots and man. The language capacity was given in order that we express love, trust, understanding and effective communication. The other capacity is, by far, more valuable and rewarding. The capacity to 'die-while-alive' is the main vehicle for true happiness, divine health, peace of mind and total freedom.

"Man, like parrot, is always in one cage or the other. He gains permanent freedom as he learns and exercises this capacity to 'die-while-alive.' Man, in his own colony, because of his attachment to things of the world, plus his unusual fear of death, chooses to forget his capacity to 'die-

Introduction

while-alive.' He is, therefore, in perpetual bondage. No cage is ever stronger than that in which individual man keeps himself. The coded message from the dead bird in the forest of Africa was intended to remind me that only as I remember to 'die-while-alive' could I gain freedom."

The parrot went on to say that it always knew that it carried that capacity; that this device was divine; and that it was there principally for personal freedom. Nowhere is bondage more prevailing than among the human colony," the parrot reiterated. To 'die-while-alive' is to mentally surrender being in need always and possessiveness. It is to surrender attachment. This is not simple at first. It requires certain mental shifts and skills that I will explain later. I will also itemize the practical usefulness and applications."

"However, back in the African woods," the parrot went on, "we have our king and the chiefs. The chiefs are the heads of the various branches. Each branch has several twigs so, we also have twig heads. The arrangement of our colony is very similar to what obtains here in your zoo but it is a lot more organized.

"If you will recollect, our Mahogany tree shapes very much like a pyramid and so should be the organization of the people in your zoo. The nest of our king is right at the top, the apex of the great tree. There are many other trees in the forest with parrots of varying numbers. Our Mahogany

Introduction

tree has the greatest number of birds; our birds are the happiest, healthiest and the most pleasant of all the birds in the forest. We have more grains in individual nests and our tree blossoms most," concluded the parrot.

"What do you suppose is the reason for the success of your colony?" enquired the hunter. "I tell you. It is principally because of the vision and resourcefulness of my king," the parrot went on. "My wise king ensures that our Mahogany tree becomes the healthiest and the tallest of all the trees. He is always talking about the importance of a great vision, and that colonies of birds, after colonies, continue to perish for lack of vision. The king sits at the top of the tree where he is able to see far and wide, and where he is able to think without hindrance. He figures out the location of the choicest seeds, the cleanest streams and the greenest palm trees for the nests.

"There are many security-alert parrots that reside around him. Such birds help keep eternal vigilance. They inform the king of any case of approaching danger; the hunters and possible attacks on our seeds from parrots invading from other colonies. The entire trunk of the tree has ten main branches. A chief has its nest at the apex of every branch. He is accountable to the king and controls the affairs in his branch.

"The branches of our tree can be likened to the

Introduction

departments of your zoo. If you take one of the big ten branches, there are ten or so twigs. Each twig is headed by an experienced and competent parrot. Again, the nest of the twig-head is at the apex of the twig. Each twig has about twelve or so nests. It is the king's order that a twig shall have no more than fifteen nests so that the twig head may coordinate effectively," concluded the parrot.

"I am getting very fascinated. It looks perfectly similar to a typical organizational structure. Suppose I use the same structure in my zoo and create no more than ten departments, divide each department into no more than ten units and have no more than 15 people per unit. My job becomes very simple. I wake up every morning to coordinate ten heads of departments, who, in turn, are trained to control ten heads of units, each of whom will finally supervise ten or so people," said the hunter.

"Yes, this will reduce your job to managing the managers," agreed the parrot. "This is very insightful, "replied the hunter. "I stop operating. I start managing. This is interesting. Tell me more," demanded the hunter.

"I was the deputy king back home," continued the parrot. "The bird that died, I suppose, must be my king. It must have missed me beyond measure. You can be sure that it would have come alive as soon as you left the colony," explained the parrot.

"Hummm," uttered the hunter. "I should have known the

Introduction

misery behind this repeated death all along. I can recollect now that I captured you in a near death circumstance."

"Yes; it was the order of my king that I died on that day one year ago, to set the entire colony free from your attack. He warned me to remember to die again upon arrival at your zoo. I forgot. Our king is very loving and protective. Like me, he had lived in a cage during his youthful days with a very wise and prosperous man called Yakubu. He got most of his wisdom and experience from this business owner. I will tell you more of this later," promised the parrot.

"Now to come to your question, each of our ten branches is respectively responsible for catching fresh worms and gathering seeds, storing water, helping the sick and handicapped birds, attacking invading birds and animals, building nests and putting the dumps at the base of our Mahogany tree as manure.

Other departments water the tree, take in new birds that seek our colony and dismiss disloyal and discordant birds. The last branch is charged with training new birds that come to the colony, along with the newly hatched birds, before they are sent to the branches where they are most suited and needed," concluded the parrot.

It was a long day of revelation. The parrot promised to share further information on the activities of their formation the following day. "It shall interest me to see you listen to the rich Yakubu on how he created his businesses that have

Introduction

continued to thrive at home and abroad, regardless of his location or involvement. For now, put my fine seed on the grass and my water nearby. I am tired and hungry," pleaded the parrot.

"I will do as you please, my beloved friend and adviser. I love you. Today is the best day of my life. I shall live to adore you and cherish your priceless contribution to my life and business," said the hunter.

The ambitious hunter was awake long before the rising of the sun the second day. The journey back from Africa, the astonishing phenomenon of 'die-while-alive' and the remarkable structure and duties of the birds in the colony fed his dreams all night.

CHAPTER ONE

A Life Of Serenity; Peace

The day's sweetest moments are at dawn!
It was another day, a glorious morning with great hope and keen expectation. Soon, the ritual of freshening up and breakfast was over. The parrot was waiting in the same position to begin from where he concluded the previous night.

"I cannot thank you enough, my wonderful friend, and now, my mentor. Good day," greeted the hunter, beaming with hilarious laughter.

"Today, I need to know more about this idea of personal freedom. How can I profit from this principle of detachment? I truly want to meet your amiable king and the rich Yakubu. I want to know all I need that I may tailor my various departments after the colony of your great king and then become very successful in India, among other zoos, as your colony has attained and sustained this giant position among other competing colonies in the forest," said the hunter.

"I greet you, my good friend and benefactor," began the parrot.

"I thank you for your wisdom and understanding. I love your spirit above all things. You desire to be rich and famous. This, to me, is a noble ambition. That you are willing to be flexible and reasonable in your approach is admirable and remarkable.

"You thirst for knowledge. You seek advancement for your zoo. You desire to be a leader among other zoos. You think like my king. You talk like the rich Yakubu. You want vision. You aim high. This is the beginning of every great achievement. Great dreams make great men. Empires are built on dreams and propelled by wisdom. Wisdom is nothing more than applied knowledge. I promise to expose you to people of knowledge. I desire to be a part of your success story.

"It shall gladden my heart to be to you, what my great king is to the rich Yakubu. I promise to be your trusted companion all the way to your position of glory. Today, I will take you through the principle of detachment, of surrender. You will learn how to let go, and let God. This is what I call 'to-die-while-alive'! I, by myself, cannot tell you all you need to know. You will follow me to my great king and meet the rich Yakubu. They shall share with you additional insights as to how you can go from here and climb onward and upward."

"Your zoo, as with everything you own today, shall belong to another person at the end of your tenure on the planet earth," remarked the parrot. "That makes perfect sense," admitted the hunter.

"If you can pretend to be dead at this time to these possessions and to mentally release rigid attachment to the outcome of all transactions; if you can simply act out your role as actors do on stage; if you can withdraw all emotional involvements, if you can surrender compulsive ownership and at the same time be effective, my great friend, you are said to 'die-while-alive'," explained the parrot.

"To pretend is to fake it," queried the hunter. "Excellent," replied the parrot. "To make it, you fake it, "continued the parrot. "Man suffers needless pains and senseless worry because of the bondage of attachment. Today, you are bonded to your zoo. You are in a cage in your own zoo. You are attached to the procedures as you are to the outcome. You feel bitter and resentful when people make mistakes or incur waste. You get agitated and upset when fewer people come to watch your animals. This is the emotional attachment you must learn to release," the parrot concluded.

The parrot then went ahead to explain to the hunter, the two general classifications of all problems. The first consisted of those you couldn't do anything about, example of this, he said, was the weather. "The very best thing one can do when it's raining is to let it rain. What you cannot help, you endure," he explained.

The other type of problems, he continued, would be those you could do something about. "Your job is to do something about such a problem without the emotion of anger, frustration, jealousy, bitterness or inferiority."

"These are negative emotions," the hunter chipped in. "Yes, you always have the capacity to put things in order without a recourse to negativity. You can step back and work on your company with a feigned attitude that it belongs to your government, you surrender ego and let go of care and worry," counseled the parrot.

"Yes. I get it. If I truly drop dead today, I will not be available to correct all annoying mistakes and the entire structure may collapse. I figure, if I stay alive, pretend to die to error of procedures and outcomes. I stay free from care and anxiety. I stay in control," admitted the hunter.

"Yes, you get the picture. You stay free. Man will not die and lay stiff as parrots do and then get himself resurrected. He, nevertheless, possesses this capacity in this manner and can exercise it at a nobler level," the parrot pointed out.

"Let me think aloud for a while, pleaded the hunter. "The entire idea will grant me peace of mind. If we agree that peace is the foundation of all enduring progress, then you are building my prosperity on a solid rock.

"The way to maximize this benefit is for me to stand back,

catch myself feeling angry or becoming resentful, and then to deliberately choose to forgive, release anger and dissolve rigid attachments to results or tasks.

"I can now choose my own attitude, regardless of what attitude I see with the people in my office. If I study my mood as if supervising myself, I can elect an uplifting mood, rather than reflect back the negative attitude or mood of other people. I can choose to be happy.

"Please, nod your head to let me know if I am thinking properly," demanded the hunter. "People who mimic the attitude of others, who become angry at angry people; who cannot forgive the mistake of employees, such people carry a great capacity to drop dead prematurely, they march rapidly towards an early grave," concluded the hunter.

"Yes. The grave is said to actually get closer to them," added the parrot. "Now, tell me more about the dangers of attachment, or the benefits of detachment. You have made me believe it has several applications and numerous gains," demanded the hunter.

"When you are attached, you are desperate about outcome. To be desperate is to repel positive outcomes. Attachment hides deep seated fear of loss. In friendship, it is the origin of possessiveness, neediness and jealousy. Jealousy is a very powerful negative emotion and, just like a strong acid, it eventually destroys its own container. It never really affects the other person. Jealousy, like the emotion of bitterness and hatred, has the capacity to drag man to the gates of hell. You see, if he drops dead, the friend or spouse he is jealous about is thereafter 'handed over' to another person. In every kind of love, there should be a certain amount of separation and detachment.

"In business activities, emotional attachment to tasks and output begets suspicion and distrust. Your job is to always have the attitude of an intelligent observer; a caring, loving and considerate manager, at all times. You will let go, even of glory, and surrender ego," advised the parrot.

"Are you preaching indifference?" asked the hunter.

"I am advocating the spirit of love; of detachment. You must know that your people are always an extension of your hands and that you are still accountable for the results. You stay in control to the degree that you stay out of rigid attachment. Your job is to share all your work among your people with the faith and trust that they can accomplish a better end than you.

"Yakubu will tell you more about the method of sharing work. My good king, thanks to Yakubu, does nothing today beyond thinking and planning. Yakubu always talked about vision; why it should be the sole responsibility of the leader and why it should be accorded a great priority," concluded the parrot.

"Is this possible? To stop working and start thinking and then to get the job done?" asked the hunter.

"Yes. Yakubu will tell you the method and gains of giving away all the responsibilities and the authority. You will then be able to see that it is only at this level that you are free from bondage. This is the only requirement that guarantees total freedom and further growth," the parrot explained further.

"Yes, to share work is called delegation. I can see that if I do not relinquish attachment, if I cannot 'die-while-alive' as you said, I would always be getting in the way of my people at work. I would nurse endless and needless concern. In fact, total detachment should be at the root of all meaningful delegation," asserted the hunter.

"You get the true picture, detachment begets freedom and control. What you compulsively possess truly possesses you, then, you are held captive, you are caged. Detachment will free man from his remaining chains.

"Surrendering is the key to true emancipation and enduring prosperity. In addition, to create a business that thrives in your absence, you will need to learn and master the art of letting your people do all the work, the entire work, in your presence."

He continued:
"I will never get a greater truth," affirmed the hunter.
"I thank you, my good friend."
"I can now envision more applications of the concept of detachment than I have ever done. Detachment is the only vehicle that can permit a pain-free giving or sharing of

work, money, food, tithe or of love. Everything I own, or will ever own, must be seen as a loan that I will one day give back to the universe. My responsibility is, therefore, to love myself and everyone in my environment without possessiveness or rigid attachment. To 'die-while-alive' is to soar above these worldly possessions. The bee does not need its wings less when it has gathered an abundant store, for if it sinks in the honey, it dies."

"You have a profound intellect," the parrot commended excitedly. "People think it is holding on that makes one strong. Most times, it is letting go," continued the parrot. "Detachment will allow you to use your zoo as a theatre or laboratory where numerous staff members come to learn and practise; where honest mistakes are allowed and where people grow and develop. As I said before, you can view your zoo as if it were a government department, where no one is indispensable, where no one suffers isolated pain arising from any unavoidable mistake. You carry this vision around and begin to act it in all your dealings.

"You will therefore sustain your serenity when a highly trained and competent worker goes. You become a captain or a coach; you don't agonize when a player goes, you simply employ a younger, quicker and better player. You train him. He again makes his contributions and later goes, and so on."

"Soldier come, soldier go, the army remains," the hunter

said jokingly. "Something like that. As your people make mistakes, they learn and grow. They gather experience and become more confident, competent, proficient, effective and resourceful. You use your zoo to grow the people rather than use the people to grow the zoo. This is the entire idea. Your zoo is no greater than the staff members. Great people, great zoo.

"Now the warning, if you cannot detach, very soon you attract sufficient negative emotion that can drag you nearer to your grave or sick bed, and any strange staff that strolls along will only need the combination of poor training and ineffective supervision to mismanage or destroy that which you have spent your entire life to create," the parrot continued.

"Yes, I agree with you," said the hunter. "I do really need to apply all these principles to my business and private life. It can confer considerable serenity and banish worry. A businessman who does not know how to conquer worry dies young. I am told that worry kills more rapidly than worms. Any more application?" demanded the hunter.

"I will give you three more," replied the parrot. "I have lived with you here for twelve months and you have talked about taking money in and out of your bank. I have never seen you talk about savings as the rich Yakubu does. Yakubu always talks of the importance of saving the first 10% of income and then detaching oneself from ownership of the money so much that it accumulates month in and month out. He always says that the money you grow in this manner will come back to grow you."

"Thank you my wise friend," responded the hunter.

"The trouble I always have with savings is leaving it there to grow for a long time. I save the money, then I 'unsave' it and then save another and so on. Detachment may be the cure I have always needed."

"Another application is in connection with negotiation. I see you negotiate with people here and feel so sorry about your approach. If you can surrender attachment to the outcome of the negotiation; if you will be willing to walk away from the negotiation table, you will have a superior power in such deals. The willingness to walk away is another way of negotiating. You lose readily in a negotiation when you are desperate, hurried, or when you become emotionally attached to the outcome," the parrot counseled.

"That is true," said the hunter.

"I am coming up with yet another insightful idea regarding the gains of sharing responsibility. I seem to be unable to dismiss it from my mind. I think that staff members' involvement will generate commitment and a sense of responsibility. I also think that commitment will give rise to job ownership and therefore, loyalty. Here in my zoo, I seem to be the only loyal person because I am the most involved; I do the most important jobs."

"Everyone becomes loyal once they have a way in the zoo to learn, grow, make mistakes, get better and make valuable contributions. When people are allowed to create something, love something, nurse something, make decisions or have a measure of control within the zoo, it then becomes a place where people derive joy, meaning, purpose and fulfillment. They don't want such a place to suffer, perish or be destroyed," said the parrot.

"Yes," agreed the hunter.

"Money or salary, though vital, is always secondary to a sense of involvement or fulfillment. If you get too attached to your zoo, if you are the only one learning and growing by deep involvement and commitment, then your attitude generally repels the needed staff loyalty. Your zealous loyalty angers the others," the parrot pointed out.

"Yes, yes, everyone becomes loyal once he has a way in the business to learn and grow, to make valuable contribution, to feel useful and hopeful," added the hunter.

"My wise king always ensures that every bird in the entire colony has a job that totally belonged to him, no matter how small. The bird is held accountable for the result of such a job. He owns the job and makes decisions on it. This is the arrangement that binds the whole colony into a highly spirited community," concluded the parrot.

The hunter thanked the parrot for the wonderful

discussion. He wished he had known about all these ideas long before he started his zoo. If the deputy to the king could reveal this much about their empire, the king himself or the rich Yakubu would certainly hand him the master key that would open every door. It has been a roller-coster experience in this 'die-while-alive' adventure. He had always been running straight after money. Equipped with the idea of detachment and people growth, he is now beginning to fall in love with the acquisition of more knowledge that will bring the needed wealth and also permit him to enjoy the money when it arrives.

He would be going back to the African forest the next day. This fresh idea of involvement can now permit him to embrace the wisdom of bringing the zoo manager along with him. They set off the next day and journeyed expectantly until they arrived at the base of the Mahogany tree.

CHAPTER TWO

How To Make People Do What You Want

The arrival of the trio - the hunter, zoo manager and the parrot was met with unusual jubilation. The entire colony of parrots went into thunderous chants and gracious songs. The deputy king must have meant a lot to this community. The joy was infectious and overwhelming. The atmosphere was electrifying.

The zoo manager could not manage his excitement and told his master, who was running happily around the Mahogany tree, that he was experiencing the happiest moment of his life. Tears of joy went down the cheek of the hunter as he admitted that he would never exchange his feelings for any form of gold or silver. He was so worked up that the rhythm of his dance out-paced the melody of the song.

Everyone was happy for different reasons. The hunter could not wait to meet the king and commence the business of flamboyant revelation he had been so lavishly promised. He was full of hope and expectation of a complete transformation and business breakthrough. The parrot was happy to be back home, while the entire colony of birds celebrated the return of their beloved deputy king.

Soon, it was time for assembly and introduction. The parrot set the ball rolling:

"My great king, I greet you. It is a thing of joy that I can be privileged to stand before you again. It calls for thanksgiving. I am grateful for your love and kindness. I thank God for your life and wisdom. My friend, the hunter, needs no further introduction. He has been very good to me in the last twelve months that I left this empire. He provided me the finest seed and showed unexpected love and unparalleled attention.

"This other fellow is the zoo manager. He is the next in command to the hunter in their organization back in India. He read about business in theory form during his youthful days.

"I have brought them here because of their desire to learn, in practical form, the organization of an empire. They wish to fashion their zoo business after the arrangement we have here in our colony and transform their career in Asia like the rich Yakubu does on the continent of Africa."

The king thanked the parrot and welcome the strangers. He narrated how his life had been very similar to that of his deputy. Several years ago, he had been caught and put in a cage by the then young Yakubu who was starting a business at the time. He stayed with Yakubu for ten years and watched as he grew in knowledge, application and prosperity.

He told the visitors that he built the first nest on the Mahogany tree ten years ago. He narrated how he had needed the knowledge and ideas he learnt during his stay with Yakubu to keep his empire flourishing.

He finally told them about Yakubu, whom, he said, had always paid monthly visits to the forest, how he had brought rare seeds and numerous gifts in his spirit of kindness and generosity. He announced that Yakubu was due to arrive the next morning.

"Today, I shall begin to share my experience with you and the rich Yakubu would take over upon his arrival," the king began.

"What should I talk about?," he demanded.

"We have talked at great length on how to 'die-while-alive.' It may be a good idea if you share a testimony or two regarding your principal role as a king and the leader of this empire," suggested the parrot.

The hunter thanked the king and got the manager to jot down every detail. He told the gathering that it was an established truth that the business of managing or governance remained essentially the same, whether it was organizing a home, a kitchen, a hotel, a hospital, a nation, a shop, a zoo or an empire of parrots.

"My commitment is to conduct the affair of my zoo after the teachings I shall be gathering in the next few days in this great forest," he continued.

He then reminded the zoo manager to put his pen to paper at all times. "Even the faintest cough of the kind king must be written," he ordered excitedly.

The king began his talk:

"My greatest job as the king is to maintain harmony in my kingdom. Peace in the animal kingdom is just as vital to progress as it is among men. Man and parrots share many attributes in common. I will explain to you, the general nature of people that I learnt during my stay with Yakubu, which has become priceless to my dealings with my fellow birds. If you know the rules and apply them, you win the game of harmony among your people. If you don't, you set yourself up for total failure.

"You need to understand the innate nature of your people, why they do what they do or why they leave undone, certain things. I shall describe thirteen general rules guiding human behaviour that you may employ to sustain peace and progress in your organizations. This, I will call, 'people skill.'

"The first rule is simple. I found out that **people are generally interested in themselves**, not in you," said the king

"Are people selfish?" asked the hunter.

"This is not selfishness. People are just that way. They are prewired to show intense interest in themselves. A simple toothache that robs you of a night's sleep shall always be of a greater concern to you than a horrific story of great disaster in a distant land.

"That is correct," admitted the zoo manager.

"How can the knowledge of this rule help us?" asked the hunter.

"You shall show intense and genuine interest in your people. This way, they will consider you very interesting and very capable of acting in their best interest. This application ties closely with the reciprocity principles. When you do what people want, they feel compelled to do what you want.

"We show interest in them first, and then, they reciprocate?," asked the hunter. "Exactly," replied the king.

"Now, how do we begin or go about showing interest in people?" asked the parrot.

"You use people words, namely, 'you and yours,' you will do away with your own words, namely, I, me, my, mine.

"People love it when you say 'you or yours,' which pertains to them. You become very boring to them when you talk about yourself as when use the other four words.

"You must talk to people about themselves, not about you. Next, you should get them to talk about themselves.

"That is insightful," said the hunter.

"I can establish, from my own life, that the times I have

secured the most friends have been the times I spend discussing about their lives, their businesses and their families; what they love and plan to do. You turn people off easily simply by bragging about yourself or your accomplishments," concluded the hunter.

"Yes. You don't take up a man's time talking about the smartness of your children; he wants to talk to you about the smartness of his children," said the king.

"It is said that anyone who loves his opinion more than his brethren, will defend his opinion and destroy his brethren," the parrot quoted.

"Your love for people must be genuine. People have great capacity to recognize fake compliments or flattery. They get turned off by any form of insincerity," advised the king.

"What is the second rule?" enquired the manager.

"People generally want to feel important," continued the king.

"Again, I cannot reiterate this enough. If you provide what people want, they will like you and do what you want," said the king.

"How do we, therefore, make people feel important?" demanded the hunter.

"You start by finding something nice to compliment in them, their dressings and accessories; use their names and pictures. People's names are the sweetest sounds to them.

They can't tire listening to their names. The best painting will forever be the picture of the person looking at it. Use people's pictures regularly.

"There are countless ways to tell the other person that you consider him or her very important. One is to show that you truly value people by appreciating their opinion.
When people ask you a question. You tactfully pause before you reply. This way, they feel that you consider their question very vital; that it is worth thinking about. It means you rate them as being intelligent, especially when you say: 'Oh that is a very wonderful question'," the king continued.

"There is a method I have used over the years that I learnt from Yakubu," the king pointed out.

"I always assume there is a sign on the chest of everyone I meet that says, *'make me feel important;'* I always heed this sign and it has won me many friends and admiration within and beyond my colony. You must always remember that people will only like you when you do what they want and they will always do what you want if they like you," reiterated the king.

"You cannot make a person feel important in your presence if you secretly feel that he is nobody. You, therefore, need to love people truthfully. Look for the good in people all the time, and sure enough, you'll find it. And as you do, say it.

"An easy way to like people is to listen to the story of their lives, their hopes and aspirations. You listen with empathy. This way, you identify with them; you truly love them. Like they say; 'when love is thick, fault is thin,'" concluded the king.

"Yes, that is a vital truth. I think the opposite is also true; when fault is thick, love is thin," echoed the hunter.

"All that will ever be important to you are your people, not the assets. Assets merely make things possible, but people make things happen," said the king.

"The third rule is that **people generally want to laugh**," continued the king.

"People want to be happy. They will give their love, support, trust and loyalty, even their business, to anyone who can make them happy.

"Laughter is a universal bond that draws all men closer. Shared laughter creates a bond of friendship. When people laugh together, they cease to be young and old, master and pupils, king and subjects, employer and employees; they become a single group of human beings enjoying their existence together.

"Laughter is the jam on the toast of life. It adds flavour, keeps it from being too dry and makes it easier to swallow. All great and sensible leaders take advantage of this. They never take themselves too seriously. They take the time to learn and perfect some sense of humour.

"When a person can no longer laugh at himself, it is time

for others to laugh at him. Leaders keep themselves motivated and happy, and as a result, they keep those around them happy and motivated as well."

"It is said in China that: 'make happy those who are near and those who are far will come,'" said the zoo manager. "Why do you need to have so many people around you?" asked the hunter.

"You will never be able to accomplish much, all by yourself. You need large numbers of willing others for you to make remarkable achievements. People buy your ideas, heed your demands, commit to your dream to the degree to which they like you and are happy with you. You will succeed in business the more you can make your people happy. In this sense, the more people you make happy, the more successful you become. Success is not simply what you do yourself; it is mainly what other people do for you.

"Take a close look at our colony here. We have the greatest collection of birds, truly happy birds happier than birds of any colony in this forest. And as a result, we are the most successful. We have more seeds, better nests, healthier birds. We sing better.

"I agree with you, great king," complimented the hunter.

"Now, make unhappy those who are near and those who are far will fly," the parrot chipped in.

"Yes," said the king.

"You need to comfort the souls of those around you. Good

manner is the art of making easy the people with whom we converse. Whoever makes the fewest people uneasy is the best breed in the company."

"Gentlemen, this is my fourth rule, **people generally love those who agree with them,**" continued the king.

"That sounds sensible," remarked the hunter, almost without thinking.

"You must, therefore, learn the art of being agreeable," replied the king.

"Any fool can disagree. The wise alone cultivates the attitude of being agreeable," said the king.

"Why do you need to be agreeable in the business place? Isn't it said that when two people always agree in one office, one of them is unnecessary?" demanded the manager.

"That is an intelligent remark," replied the king.

"There is always a place for differences in view points. The truth is that people love those who agree with them. They dislike those who argue. The art of great conversation consists, as much, in listening politely, as in talking agreeably.

"You will always need the cooperation and support of your people. They will be more inclined to say, yes, when they like you. And people never like those who argue. They love agreeable managers. To be agreeable is to be tactful. Tact is that rare ability to keep silent while two friends are arguing and you know both of them are wrong.

"Yes, if you truly want people to get along with you, simply get along with them," added the parrot.

"We should tell them we agree with them. To do this, nod your head. Say, 'I agree with you; that to me is an intelligent idea; that is reasonable, and so on," said the king.

"What if we don't agree with them? Some ideas are damn stupid," insisted the hunter.

"The rule is simple. You keep quiet," replied the king.

"It is unwise to tell people you disagree with them. Always refrain from arguing. All you generate is heat. If you always win all your arguments, then you always lose all your friends," added the parrot.

"We are taught in school to practise the 101% principles," said the zoo manager. "What is that about?" asked the parrot.

"That we find the one thing we agree on with another person and then give 100% of our encouragement," replied the manager. "Excellent," commented the king.

"That is the idea. You simply ignore what you don't agree with. The truth is that people have a way of becoming what you encourage them to be, not what you nag them to be. The few who are lifting the world upward and onward are those who encourage more than criticize. Encouragement is food for the heart, and every heart is a hungry heart," concluded the king.

"And this takes us to rule number five, **people generally want to talk.**"

"What is the benefit of talkatives in the business place?" asked the hunter.

"Yes. Good question. The lesson from this is the need for you to learn to listen. Listening builds trust and trust is the pillar of every form of relationship.

"A good listener is better than a good talker in affection rating," added the parrot.

"Yes," agreed the manager.

"We were told in school that the English Language has the same set of letters for listen and silent," commented the hunter.

Everyone laughed.

"Yes. To listen, be silent," continued the king.

"God gave each man two ears and one mouth so that he listens twice as much as he talks."

"I agree with you, the great king. But if everyone begins to listen, to whom will they listen?" asked the zoo manager.

There was laughter again. "Let me take you back to the rule. People generally want to talk. You will never run out of talkers. Listeners are always in short supply," continued the king.

"Parrots are noted for being good talkers. To lead among them, the approach must be different. Become a good listener."

"That is a wonderful stuff," said the hunter.

"But isn't it said that, 'silence is foolish if we are wise, but wise if we are foolish?" asked the hunter.

"Yes, the question is, how do you know you are wise? A person who thinks himself wise is often the most foolish. It is really unwise to be too sure of one's wisdom.

It is easier to talk. Great talkers are everywhere. We have to learn to listen, that way, we learn to lead. It takes a person about two years to learn how to talk, and the rest of his life, to learn when not to. No one has a better command of the language than the person who keeps his mouth shut. He always has the questions, and as a result, he always has the control," said the king.

"Great. How do we listen?," asked the hunter.

"Let me tell you the classic approach," began the king.

"You look at the person who is talking.

"Always better to sustain eye contact.

"You lean towards the speaker and listen attentively? You ask questions; this is flattery. You stick to the speaker's subject and resist the temptation to interrupt. You use the speaker's words — you and yours.

"Always pretend you never knew whatever they tell you, even if they are talking about the same story the tenth time," the king concluded.

"Very thought provoking," commented the zoo manager.

"Quite insightful," said the hunter.

"Now, let me take you to rule six; **people generally act on motives,**" continued the king.

"You must remember this rule everyday of your lives. If you want people to take any form of action, you must supply the motive. No one ever acts without motives. Now, listen. This is vital. The motive for such an action must always be to the benefit of the person or he will not take the action," added the king.

"That sounds like rule one," commented the hunter.

"Yes. You are thinking. Self interest is the origin of every form of motivation to action," said the king.

"To get people to do what you want them to do, you must think of the benefit in it for them. If you must assign a job to a person, your own duty is to begin by finding out what will encourage the person to do it and then you figure out how to expose this benefit long before you invite him for the job. The way I go about doing it is simple. I ask of myself. Will doing this job make this person grow in cash, knowledge, wisdom, exposure, pride, ego, recognition, approval or fulfillment? Will doing this job ultimately make this person happy? You can be sure that no one will get committed in any sort of activity without a self-serving motive; it is human nature to want. People want. They desire. You must either give people what they want or persuade them to want what you've got. This way, you can go ahead to demand and encourage them to supply what you want.

"This is a remarkable idea. If this is all I come here to get, it is much more than worth it," said the hunter.

"Rule number seven is that **people are generally skeptical**," continued the king.

"What does that mean?" asked the hunter.

"People generally don't believe you. They are doubtful of your intention. They are always not sure whether or not you are representing their true interest," answered the king.

"What then do we do? Convince them or persuade them?" the hunter demanded.

"Yes. You figure out a way to persuade them. One way is to add credibility to your message. To do this, you can speak through the third person. Better if the third person is an authority figure or a credible person.

"You may come up with a quotation that favours your point of view. The person quoted may or may not be present. For example, when asked if your zoo is a good place to work in, you don't just say 'yes; this will only fuel more doubt or arouse greater suspicion. Instead, you say something like this, 'In the last ten years, no employee has left us to work in another establishment. My staff members always remark that the zoo is the best place to work in.' In essence, the employees are answering for you," the king replied.

"Oh my God!," exclaimed the zoo manager.

"I used this same rule to secure my current employment but

never knew I was following a rule. I was asked at the interview if I felt I could do the job well. I simply replied that: 'My past employer loved my way of doing this kind of job'," concluded the zoo manager.

"Yes. It sounds more convincing when you quote people, relate success stories, cite facts and statistics."

"Now let us go to rule number eight," invited the king. **"People are generally confused,"** the king revealed. Everyone laughed.

"Don't get me wrong," pleaded the king.

"Most people cannot make up their minds most of the time."

"So, we help them make up their minds," guessed the hunter.

"Yes. You got it," replied the king.

"When you suggest that they take action or buy something, they are not sure whether to say 'yes or no."

"Suppose I want them to say yes?" asked the hunter.

"That is the logical question. I will relate four main approaches," the king replied.

"First, give reasons for people to say yes. It must be their reasons, not your reasons. The reason must be to their benefit and advantage. Tell them how they will profit from your suggestion or proposal.

"The second approach; ask 'yes' questions. These are questions that can only be answered with a yes. The

purpose of this is to set up a pattern of letting them say 'yes' by suggesting the benefit of your proposal. Here are a few examples. 'You want your family to be happy?
You want the original?
You want to stay healthy?
You want to be rich?'
Always nod your head as you ask these questions. They are more likely to say yes answers when you nod your head.

"The third approach, my dear friends, is to give people a choice between two yes answers and never a choice between 'yes' or 'no.'
Again, here are some typical questions you pose.
'Will blue or brown be okay?
We meet in school or hostel?
You start tomorrow or Monday?
You pay in cheque or cash?'

"My fourth and final approach is psychological. It is always to expect people to say yes to you, and then let them know you expect them to say yes," the king continued.
'That is quite a mouthful" remarked the zoo manager.
"Thank you, the great manager, rule number nine is that **people generally reciprocate the behaviour of others.** They are prewired to pay you back for anything you do to or for them," the king explained.

"How can this be of help?" asked the hunter.
"I have said once that this principle is the foundation of all

the rules, if you demonstrate that you dislike people, they simply dislike you," retorted the king.

"So we let them know that we like them," said the hunter.

"Yes. You do that. They will only do what you want them to do if they know that you like them and are acting in their best interest," stressed the king.

"You must be sincere at all times. I cannot stress this enough. People soon find out your true intention. Yakubu always say that the first few seconds of meeting people set the tone of the eventual relationship. He often advises people to bear this in mind.

"He has a formula for this. Since people always reciprocate your behaviour, when you meet a person for the first time, you establish eye contact and then give a sincere, generous smile. What you put out to others, is what you get right back.

"A smile is the shortest distance between two people. The smile and the eye contact generate an initial bond, almost immediate chemistry.
The key lies in the timing. The smile should come before you start the greeting. This sets the stage for a warm and friendly mood," concluded the king.

"Now, my great king, suppose I am not in the mood to smile," asked the hunter.

"You can put yourself in the mood by saying 'cheese' inaudibly. It works. Actions always precedes emotions.

Smiling is gracious. The smile that lights the face will also warm the heart; it gets people excited before you utter a word."

"A common application of this reciprocity principle is to do a favour for people. I am not talking about bribery or any dubious attempt to manipulate others. When you do a favour for people, they are internally propelled to rid themselves of this indebtedness. Often, they can return your favour in a measure far in excess of your original favour.

"We have four more rules to go," reminded the king.

"Rule number ten is that **people are generally thirsty for praise.**

"To be liked, you must be generous with your praise. Always find something to praise in the other person, and then, do it.

"In praising people, there are certain rules you must keep in mind. Again, as with all people related rules, you must be sincere. You will praise only the act and not the person. Praising the act creates incentive for more of it but praising the person breeds suspicion, embarrassment or awkwardness.

"Rather than say Yakubu is a nice man, you say: 'Yakubu has shown kindness and thoughtfulness in bringing plenty seeds to the colony of birds every month in the last ten years.'

"Again, you make the praise specific, immediate, and

finally, you praise in public, if possible."

There was a pause, and then the manager looked straight at the king, smiled and began. "You are indeed a great and wise ruler. I have profited more in the last hour of your teaching than in all the combined hours of lectures in my three years of university education. I was told in school that more than 80% of happiness always derive from people and relationships, yet, no one ever took the pain to nurse me the needed people skills. If every youth is made to undergo your lessons, the family environment, the offices and the entire society will experience stupendous joy, serenity and progress. I consider myself extremely fortunate to sit here and listen to your ageless wisdom and timeless teachings. I thank you, the great king," concluded the manager.

"It is my privilege," responded the king.

"You really make me feel good. Our greatest pleasure is always that which rebounds from hearts one has made glad. I truly appreciate your comments," the king added.

"The eleventh rule is that **people generally do not love criticism, opposition or blame,**" continued the king.

"So we should never criticize people?" enquired the hunter.

"If we must criticize people, we should do that without arousing resentment," counseled the king. You must know that worse than the sin you criticize is the sin of criticizing. If and when criticism or blame becomes inevitable, it must be conducted in private. This way, you minimize bitterness," continued the king.

"You invite the person, close the door, ensure there is no listener and speak in low voice. You start with a kind word.

"Yes," interrupted the manager.

"It is called, 'kiss them before you kick them,' continued the manager.

Everyone laughed.

"This approach creates a friendly atmosphere," continued the king.

"Like in the praise, always criticize the act, not the person. This makes it impersonal.

"Your job is to say what is not done well and then to supply the right way to do it.

Always ask for cooperation, don't demand it. Appeasing is a thousand times better than commanding. Commanding should be the last resort.

"And finally, be sure you offer no more than one criticism per offence. You generate no chains. Never refer to previous errors. You always finish the reprimand on a friendly note. You say: 'You have always been one of our best hands, we are together, we both benefit' and so on.

"Of praise and criticism, this truth you must acknowledge; if your aim is to criticize, you must remember to praise; if your aim is to praise, you must forget to criticize, concluded the king.

"Thank you, the wise king," said the hunter.

"The sun is up and the hunger is here. I suggest we tidy up the last two rules before lunch," the hunter advised.

"At the twelveth position is the rule that **people generally love to be thanked**," began the king.

"We need to thank people. It is said that God has two dwellings: One in heaven, and the other in a meek and thankful heart. Everyone seems to have daily requirement for thanks, as they do for vitamins. Many people suffer thanks deficiency, they have not been thanked for years," everyone laughed again.

"I figure there must be a skillful way to thank people, as in praise and reprimand," said the hunter, looking straight at the king.

"Yes, I know you'll say this," continued the king.

"First, you must know that it is not enough for you to feel grateful. It is important that you say it.

"Second, you should thank the act. You get more of what you thank. We lose the chance of getting more of the things we fail to thank; people cannot read your mind. Always remember to tell people when you feel thankful and then, why you feel thankful.

"Third, when you say, 'thank you,' you must mean it. Sincerity is priceless. People can always tell a fake from a genuine gratitude. When you express gratitude, do that gladly, clearly and distinctly. Feel happy as you say, 'thank you.'

"Fourth, you will look at the person you thank. This means a lot. Anyone worth thanking is worth looking at. Maintain eye contact, if possible. This adds more power.

"Fifth, thank people by name, 'Peter, thank you,' is better than just a plain 'thank you.'

"Finally, you must work hard at thanking people; hibernate, catch people needing to be thanked, always watch for chances to say 'thank you; you will never find a greater asset in human relations that surpasses the willingness and the ability to have the attitude of gratitude and to express it openly, at all times," concluded the king.

"Thank you, the great king," chorused everyone.

"The last rule must be a powerful one," guessed the hunter.

"The last rule is pivotal. Before I tell you, I must remind you that you will always need loyal, supportive and loving people around you all the days of your life. You will always need their help. There is very little, if anything, you can do by yourself for yourself," hinted the king.

"That is very true," agreed the hunter.

"The last rule is this: **People generally love and hang around those who keep their temper**," began the king.

"Tolerance is the ultimate rule in all your affairs with people. Mildness always governs more than anger. It is the greatest manifestation of power to be calm.

"The fact is that, it is unwise to lose one's temper. Bad temper is its own scourge. Few things are more bitter than to feel bitter. A man's venom poisons him more than his victim," the king explained.

"Those with a good sense restrain their anger, they earn esteem by overlooking wrongs," quoted the hunter.

"Anger is just one letter short of danger," added the zoo manager.

"And whatever begins in anger ends in shame; anger and argument are indeed true cousins," said the parrot.

"You really cannot put valuable ideas across by getting cross," continued the king. "You need tolerance. Intolerance robs you of joy, surrounds you with unpleasantness and repels people, joy, peace and prosperity. Temper is wild; tame it, keep it, and kill it," concluded the king.

"I must thank you very much, my great king," said the hunter.

"My good friend and mentor, the parrot, had spoken to me about the idea of detachment, that it holds the key that locks the door to negative emotions of hatred, jealousy, bitterness and anger."

"You 'die-while-alive,'" said the king.
Everyone laughed.

CHAPTER THREE

The Fire Of Desire

The hunter and his zoo manager spent the entire evening building a tent that would represent their own nest during their stay in the forest. The next day was considered very crucial. The wealthy Yakubu would be arriving to share his extraordinary testimony and wealth of experience.

Yakubu arrived at dawn as expected, on a horse which carried a huge cart. The zoo manager and his boss, who were delighted to meet him, had to help with off-loading the contents of the cart; bags of seeds, sealed buckets of water, lamps, camping gas, burners and numerous other stuff.

It was ceremony time again in this glorious colony. Songs of praise and appreciation rent the air. There was a harmonious blend of native African hymns with some Hindi collections. The joy knew no bounds.

Soon, it was business time and all was quiet again. The king broke the ice. "I say good morning to all of you. We have a great day on our hands. The sun is kind and the weather is pleasant. We have in our midst the patron of our empire.

"He was first seen here two decades ago with a little cage and some delicious bait. I was quite young, naive and hungry. I rushed for the tasty stuff and was caught. You might laugh at the folly of biting at the bait of pleasure without considering the possibility of a hook! There seems to be a divine reason for every occurrence.

"He took me away for five years, during which I witnessed the creation of his first business enterprise. He had been to the university to learn some trade and the knowledge so gained didn't seem to answer the great proportion of his nagging problems.

"I can still remember those days; he would arise before dawn with books in search of business solutions. Today, he is made. He owns a great telecom house that has connection to most African nations. He is the president of the largest network of fast food chains in Africa. He is loaded with great business ideas and stirring principles; gentlemen join me to welcome our dear friend and benefactor, the rich Yakubu."

There was an applause which seemed to last forever, an applause that started from the hunter and his manager and then got echoed and reverberated endlessly among the entire colony of the grateful birds.

"The great king, I thank you for your love and

thoughtfulness. I can confess here today that I have gained more from my visit to your empire than you have profited from my grains," began Yakubu.

"It has always been an inspiration to be here among your subjects, the soul soothing songs, the serene and quiet woods have been, altogether, a priceless treasure."

He then turned to the hunter and the zoo manager.

"I greet you, friends from Asia. You are welcome to Africa. The village of my birth is just a few distance away. I was once as hungry for this kind of knowledge as you now desire. Today, I seem to be hungrier. The appetite that began like a few thread has encompassed me today like a mighty cable.

"I come to this forest every month, without fail, in the past two decades. I get away from the confusion of the city and the complication and intricacies of the business environment and spend two days among these pleasant parrots. In this silent, serene wilderness, the weary can regularly gain a heart-bath in perfect peace.

· I delight to steal away for two or three days together, every month, and bathe my spirit in the freedom of the old woods, and to grow young again. I like to steep my soul in a sea of quiet, with nothing floating past me but the perfume of flowers and soaring birds, and shadows of clouds.

"Perhaps, you would say, it would be a good idea, for people in the city to muffle every telephone, stop every vehicle, and halt every activity for one hour, some day, just to give people a chance to ponder for a few minutes on what it is all about; why they are living and what they really want.

"Every month, I come here with paper and pen and three fundamental enquiries. The quiet forest and the wisdom of the king have rendered incalculable value. My three questions have remained the same over the years, but the answers have continued to change.

"My first soul searching question is this: 'What exactly am I trying to do with my life?' I put all answers that come to mind on paper. I rub minds with the king and derive counsel from his ancient wisdom.

"The first question is the foundation of the next, which is,' how am I trying to do it?' I take several hours writing away my usual approach. And now, the last question: 'Could my approach be wrong?' Or, put another way, 'could there be a better way?' This is where the rubber meets the road. I have been privileged to search my mind, to invite my soul, to figure out, without distraction, all possible ways. Sometimes, I harvested some remarkable breakthrough ideas, simply by considering new ways, better steps, simpler methods, cheaper plans, easier channels and faster routes. I reap ideas.

"The appearance of an idea is like that of a loved one. We imagine that we shall never forget it and that the beloved can never become indifferent to us; but out of sight, out of mind! The finest thought runs the risk of being irretrievably forgotten if it is not written down. The palest ink is said to be better than the sharpest memory. I commit all ideas to paper.

"I have never been too carried away by the quality of fresh ideas I generate. Often, I question my basic assumptions. In all affairs, business and personal; it's a healthy thing, now and then, to hang a big question mark on the things we've long taken for granted. Experience has since taught me that if a great plan exists, a thorough search or some deeper thought might unearth a greater one.

"Friends from Asia, I am impressed with your appetite for knowledge. I will do no more than tell you tales on how learning has brought me this far. Every man who knows how to read has it in him, the power to magnify, to multiply the ways, in which he exists, to make his life full, significant and interesting.

"Building a business structure is similar to farming. On the farm, you plant a seed, water the soil and add some manure. The seed grows into some mighty structure and produces a particular form of harvest that is identical to the nature of the seed. In the process of growth, weeds come in to undermine the harvest. A reasonable farmer that loves his plant and treasures the harvest must hate the weeds.

"In business, like the seed, you generate an idea that

carries some commercial values. You build a structure similar to the form of the tree. Here, you don't need water and manure. You need people, their ideas and efforts. You therefore invite competent people who, in your wisdom, will be suitable working within such a structure and capable of generating the desired harvest or profit. Many of your people will nourish the growth and multiply the harvest. A few of them, though well meaning, and right thinking, may harm the structure and undermine the profit. Like the farmer, you shall remove all incompetent people and bring in more wealth creators.

"Today, I want to tell you about the nature of business structures that you may generate an unstoppable drive to build one by yourself for yourself. I want to wet your appetite," Yakubu concluded his introductory speech.

"Thank you, Yakubu, for your moving testimony," said the king.

"Gentle words, quiet words, are, after all, the most powerful words. They are more convincing, more compelling, more prevailing. Your words have got me thinking very vigorously. The structure of our Mahogany tree here and the structure of your business empire could carry some hidden semblance.

"I have been thinking. There seems to be some hidden incentives and benefits for business starters, for those who choose to begin where they are with what they have. They seem to put themselves on the side of the angels. The very few people who act promptly on the urge to create, who learn and grow, seem to end up at the top. They do all the work at the beginning and thereafter, progressively work less as more people arrive. The structure of every organization, regardless of the starter, seems to favour a particular arrangement. People at the top seem to work less and earn more; those at the bottom, in contrast, work harder and earn less?

"I feel there may be some divine call, almost a relentless and inaudible shout for people to start something, and then to begin to climb and keep climbing away from the bottom to the top. There seem to be some divine penalty for those who fail to heed the call to climb. The tool for climbing, as I have come to realize, is learning. The more you learn, the less you have to physically work, and the more you earn. Could refusal to learn and grow be a great sin that carry such heavy penalty of misery and penury?

"Let me illustrate this with the structure of the tree that carries this empire. The base of this tree carries all the weight of the tree, branches, twigs, leaves, nests, seeds, water and the birds. It is also saddled with the yoke of burrowing into the hard soil to get water and minerals that are carried through the trunk to the young green leaves for food preparation. The leaves prepare the food, retain a greater proportion and then send the crumbs down to flow through the trunk until only a fraction gets to the overly hardworking roots and base of the tree.

"I am worried about the presence, or otherwise, of fairness. The topmost enjoys the most spoils, does the least work and have the most support, the base does the most work and has the least benefits. Yakubu, is this the way you have with your business structure? Can wisdom emerge from this consideration?" demanded the king.

"I thank you, my great king," began Yakubu.
"This is precisely what I discovered within the structure of the human society that has made me pay recurrent homage to this retreat in the last twenty years. Like this tree, the human society has the basic pyramidal structure. It is called the socio-economic pyramid. It has a flat large base and a pointed narrow apex and everyone alive resides and works at his portion of this pyramid.

"The bottom layer is populated by the poor, the children, the beggars, the borrowers and sorrowers. Certain people, for one thousand and one very legitimate reasons, remain here all the days of their lives. As they have no means of livelihood, they depend for their survival on the benevolence and generosity of the people in the upper layers. They live on crumbs.

"Now, don't get me wrong. There may be some divine purpose for this arrangement. I was right at these bottom layers at the time of finishing school. I needed support. My turning point came during one of my visits to this great retreat. I laid awake here and then suddenly, I perceived a ladder, though invisible, a real ladder that leads to the upper layers.

"How could I climb? The first innocent approach was to keep learning. I began. The more I studied and applied, the higher I climbed. As I climbed, I began to see an ever-increasing level of benefits. I then decided to commit to climbing, all the days of my life. My dear friend, knowledge is the ladder.

"I can confirm to you here today that the top 5% of the population that work and reside at the apex of this pyramid have more than 70% of the entire wealth in the society. The large 95% of the people at the lower layers share a meagre 30%. It is a tremendous incentive to belong to this top 5% category and remain there all the days of one's life. The truth is that anyone who has sufficient desire and determination, anyone with the right proportion of motive, can climb high and as a result, be a blessing to all the rest.

"Now, get this fact. Just as the green leaves in the king's metaphor are not safe if they prepare the food and fail to send down some portions for the trunk and the roots, many wise people at the top of this pyramid are fast beginning to discover that their health, security and longevity are attained and sustained to the extent that they open up to banish poverty, diseases and ignorance among the people in the lower layers. They need to help others to do the needed climbing. To stay happy, they must help people in the lower layers to recognize the ladder; they must encourage the people to commit to climbing.

"How come we have this strange arrangement?, enquired the hunter.

"As you speak, I also saw similarity with the human structure. The legs that carry the weight, pound the streets and do the most work have the poorest supply of blood and nutrients; the head that is always suspended in air, that enjoys eternal support also gets the richest blood supply, the best nutrients, the highest oxygen and the quickest repair in case of injury. My dear Yakubu, is this not worrisome?"

"I think we should allow Yakubu to go on," urged the zoo manager.

"I want to see as quickly as possible where I belong. As you can see, every organization, private or government, has this arrangement. Our zoo back in India has the top directors, middle level managers and the general workers. The directors and managers are few but earn by far more than the vast general employees who do the most work. I learnt in Pareto Principle that in any organization, be it government or private, the top 20% earn 80% of the available salary, while the bottom 80%, who work the hardest, share a meagre 20%. Why? Yakubu, get going. I have my pen handy and my paper tidy," concluded the zoo manager.

"Thank you gentlemen," Yakubu began again.

"You know, everyone at the top was once at the bottom. One day, he made up his mind that he must end the stressful life he was living; the misery and suffering at the bottom. Then, he began to search for the handles and then to take some steps. He discovered that certain price must be paid. There seems to be no gain without pain.

"God, in His infinite wisdom, must have surrounded man with all manners of painful necessities that he may have sufficient motive to do a quick climb away from the arena of misery. The tragedy is that only very few people take some personal responsibility for such a climb. Majority feel comfortable to blame friends and neighbours for their situations. They get attached to the notion that the people in the upper layers owe them a living. You can be sure that as long as there are people to blame, an able bodied man will stubbornly remain stuck to the bottom of the socio-economic pyramid. Taking personal responsibility for their lives and fortune is the first requirement that opens the doorway for effective upward climb.

"Let me also add that it may be unfair to blame every resident of the bottom layers, inspite of the hardship and overcrowding. Perhaps, no one ever told them of the tremendous capacity for achievement that is possible for them, if only they could be shown the way and persuaded to put some efforts. Majority do wait until they finally come to terms with the truth that their major responsibility in life is to succeed; that as adults, no one may be there to hold their hands, that heaven is designed for him that helps himself and that the kingdom of hell is always prepared for the rest.

"One day, one by one, at different moments, people get the idea that the top is possible, less competitive and more desirable, then, they wake up to a burning desire. A desire to try. And as they do, they make the needed decision, a solemn and resolute decision to climb. Beyond this, the will power and discipline they need begin to develop.

"The good news is that not all the people remain at the bottom all the days of their lives. My great king and beloved friends, permit me to put aside the subject of structure that we may find time to complete the testimony of today," said Yakubu

"You have our blessing," said the king.

"My turning point came one afternoon. I was working at a big desk with a great bank at the time. It dawned on me that there was a huge demand for fast food at lunch time for all categories of workers. I went home greatly consumed with this idea.

"I could not sleep that night. My mind raced rapidly through the gamut of bachelors and spinsters that could queue in their hundreds, waiting for me to cure their hunger and quench their thirst. I felt very strongly that I could do it. I

The Fire Of Desire

saw at the time that a few restaurants existed, but I could also see the great opportunity for newcomers with fresh drive, some unique and beneficial approach.

Every great business, as I have come to realize, begins with an idea. A small idea that grows and sprouts through an intense fire of desire," concluded Yakubu.

CHAPTER FOUR
Creating An Enduring Business System

"It is not my desire to run you through all my trials, tribulations and triumphs," began Yakubu.

"You will definitely benefit more if I counsel you today based on my accumulated experience. When you come up with a viable business idea, your next job is to nurse a sustained desire to win. You expect to succeed. This soon develops into an intense passion that grants imagination. Controlled imagination is the source of all forms of motivation.

"You need to take your idea into the theatre of imagination. To know is nothing, to imagine is everything. If you can imagine it, then you can achieve it. Every great advancement in business has emanated from a new audacity of imagination.

"You will, therefore, demand of yourself, 'where will this idea lead in the next fifty years?' This is a guided attempt to see the invisible," Yakubu said.

"Getting a vision," said the parrot.

"Yes. Comprehending the finish line and moulding it the

way you desire; putting the end in view," responded Yakubu.

"A good vision consists of being able to see the trees and the forest. A great vision comes in advance of any task well done. It is the Aladdin's lamp of the soul; the divine spark that lights the lamp of progress.

"Vision is vital; it foretells what may be ours. It is an invitation to do something. With a great mental picture in mind, we go from one accomplishment to another, using the materials about us only as stepping stones to that which is higher and better and greater and more satisfying.

"You begin creating your vision by examining the industry the idea will fit into. Could it be banking, education, transportation, agriculture, eatery, hospitality, manufacturing, construction, engineering, health, oil and gas, information, publishing, mass media and so on.

"You conduct every preparation of this sort with a pen and paper. It will help your thinking if you can determine the current champions in the industry. Their position can aid your imagination. Pay a visit to their factory or showroom; do some research. Create a personal library on the industry; read the books. The more you know in such area, the more you grow, and the less you fear. You grow to love the industry; you generate intense desire and then, passion.

"Now, this is vital; how will your imagination assist in moving you from the idea stage into the position of the current champion or beyond? You write down all the various steps you can take, even though you may have no financial muscle at this time. Writing lends clarity and confers a higher level of self-belief. It puts you on the driver's seat. You feel in charge.

"You will come up with a business name that is simple, easy to recall, and if possible, revealing and impactful," concluded Yakubu.

"Tell them they need to think big," said the king.

"Thank you, my great king," continued Yakubu.

"Like the king has suggested. You shall not bargain with life for a penny! You must stretch your imagination beyond the elastic limit. You will feel great to the extent that your ideas are magnificent. Since you will be required to think, it is well worth it to think really big. This brings tremendous motivation, which cultivates the needed passion and enthusiasm. It is at this level that inspiration begins to creep in. Your writing must also include the benefit of the products or services of your anticipated company to yourself, your staff members, the society, the customers and the immediate community," concluded Yakubu.

"Now, I have a nagging question," said the hunter.

"I really don't know what to do. I have never come up with this level of thinking and writing all my life. I have been running my zoo ferociously and impulsively for twelve years. How do I accommodate the application of this new knowledge? Is it not terribly late?" asked the hunter.

Yakubu laughed and responded.

"It is certainly not late. You just go ahead and begin your writing today, taking your current situation as the starting line and stretching your imagination and writing into the next fifty years. Your jottings or plans will demand of you, constant review and upgrade, on a regular basis, as the years go by," replied Yakubu.

"Less they think the writing is over, I suppose you let them define the character of the company they want to create," directed the king.

"Thank you, my wise king," continued Yakubu.

"This will bring us to the subject of values. Ask yourself and put the answer down on paper; what are your basic fundamental values as an individual? These are the values you treasure in yourself and cherish in others. Could it be honesty, hard work, humility, tenacity, boldness, courage, passion, determination, integrity, perseverance, charity, incremental improvement, cleanliness, diligence, caring and loving attitude, innovation or excellence? This list could be endless.

"Next, itemize such values you think could ensure a harmonious and effective running of the company from now and beyond the fifty-year margin. How can you marry your personal values and those of the anticipated company? Lastly, shortlist the values to the bearest minimum for easy remembering, effective application and

Creating An Enduring Business System

continuous enforcement. You may come up with a list of say, three to nine basic values," concluded Yakubu.

"This is a lot of preparation," remarked the zoo manager.

"Yes. Preparation is the key to winning," replied Yakubu.

"Let me take you to the most exciting bit; the mission statement.

"In practical terms, the mission statement is a vehicle; it comes up as an inspiring sentence that spells the benefits of your company by employing the values to achieve the desired vision.

"The values make the business idea achievable, at least, on paper," said Yakubu.

"The people in the company shall need to work the values as a way of life in order to achieve the desired goal of the organization," added the king.

"Thank you, my king," continued Yakubu.

"You will make your sentence short, sharp, lean and muscular.

"My wise king, friends from Asia, this is where we are coming," continued Yakubu.

"You will have to sell your vision to others who will work with you in the company. Your job is to make them identify with you. They will understand and treasure the promise in your dream before they can demonstrate any form of involvement or commitment.

"You can only sell to people who are willing and able. This is the basic truth in all selling. You need people to come on board. Only those who can see such invisible goals can go on to accomplish the desired outcome.

"You will therefore ensure that you start off by hiring the right people. This is said to be the first law of management. The right people are always those who are willing and able to buy and implement your values, mission and vision.

"Tomorrow, I shall be taking you through the great ways to hire great people. Long before your people arrive, you will establish the benefit of your vision to them and their lives; you spell what is in it for them. People only buy benefits. You need to convince yourself of how your organization will make the people get better, happier and richer. How will they grow in your company? Your business must make them feel great. How can you accomplish this end?

"It will also help if you can determine, in your imagination, where the pioneering people will be in the scheme in five, ten, twenty and fifty years. Will they grow, for instance, to become managers and directors with official cars, residential quarters and have buoyant remuneration? Is this position achievable? How convinced are you? This shall determine how convincing you can be.

"Where will you be doing the selling of your vision and mission? Meetings, notice boards, inspirational messages,

Creating An Enduring Business System

company anthems?; repeat exposure and adherence to your mission statement may come handy as tenable sites. Your job of selling the invisible is only complete when your people can take ownership of the vision; when they feel: 'This is our mission.' Even at that, you still need to continue further reinforcement in order to ensure that they stay focused and happy all along the way.

"You will need to establish that the personal goals and dreams of your people, their desires and aspirations, can be accomplished within the organization. If not, it should be a rung on the ladder towards where they want to end up in life. What I always emphasize to beginners in business is to conduct their thinking and planning as though they were already big and running a fifty year old conglomerate. This attitude alone has proved to accelerate progress far more assuredly than any single factor," concluded Yakubu.

"I thank you, Yakubu," said the hunter.

"All your narration has served to fuel a strong desire to win deep within my soul. You have broadened my thinking and perspectives about the whole essence of planning. You start by talking about structure. My question now is this, how does one put together an enduring organizational structure?" asked the hunter.

"Thank you for your observation," continued Yakubu.

"The organogram is to the organization what the socio-economic pyramid is to the society. The entire idea is to get the organization well coordinated."

"Yakubu, I will have to come in at this stage," interrupted the king.

"We must do away with all the big grammar that promises much and delivers little. Our friends here are not strict scholars, they are practical men. They want only the meat in the pie. Please, spare them the loaf.

"Yakubu, tell them only such things that they can put on their paper, that can transform their fortunes. Another day, we can play with the theory, "the king continued.

"Thank you, the great one," began Yakubu.

"Back at home, my company has me as the Chairman. This role puts me at the apex of the pyramid of our company structure. We have seven members as board of directors. Each of them heads different geographical zones where our business influence and offices penetrate.

"Now, within each zone, there are about seven to ten branches. Each of these branches is headed by a Branch Manager who coordinates the affairs of eight to twelve units. Each unit is in turn headed by a Supervisor who takes charge of the activities within his unit; the unit is made up of not more than ten people.

"The main purpose of having this structure mapped out is to come up with job description for each cadre. You will also need to mention the key result areas in those jobs. If the Chairman has twelve main assignments, the key result areas are such activities that he alone has the capacity to do most effectively, that if done really well, will make significant effect on the progress of the company.

"In my own company, apart from the job description for each staff and the key result areas, it is mandatory for each staff member to have, at least, a particular job that belongs to him or her. This has helped us to involve everyone and assist us to achieve peer monitoring and supervision.

"We treat each unit as a team in a soccer match. The role of the striker, midfielder, defender or goalkeeper is well defined. We, however, realize that a chain is no stronger than its weakest link. We serve each other in order that the success of the team is accorded priority."

"Now, Yakubu," broke in the zoo manager.
"What if the company is not so large as yours? Suppose the entire company is made up of a humble lady with a sales girl in her little shop. How do you draw up the organogram?" he demanded.

"That is a thoughtful question," responded Yakubu.
"Her kind of company is called, Sole Proprietorship. The structure is exactly what you have described. It is different from those of partnership, limited liability companies and those of public limited liability companies.

"It is the order of the king that we save the terminologies and reduce the entire essence to issues of practical usefulness. The chief reason we develop the organogram is

Creating An Enduring Business System

to lay out a frame that the various job descriptions, the administrative hierarchy, could be properly articulated.

"Now, if you start off as a sole trader, you must establish what your main duties are. If you conduct such duties diligently and effectively and care for your customers, large clients will come knocking, vacancies will open up, as you will probably not be able to handle all the growing number of customers. If this trend continues to gather momentum, your staff strength will get larger.

"You will always need to gradually organize your people and their roles in a graded order as described above, spelling the responsibilities, as well as the authorities," concluded Yakubu.

"You have just described my precise situation when I was the only parrot on this Mahogany tree," recalled the king.

"The tree was quite little at the time. My nest was right at the middle and there were no branches as we have them today. Soon the tree began to grow taller and new birds began to arrive. I never accommodated any of them until I had a special and specified duty ready for them to do.

"As the branches developed and the number of birds increased, the most experienced bird was accorded the task of branch head. Every bird had its role and knew it in detail. In addition, every bird had a superior officer whom it had to impress, who acted as the boss and determined its future within the colony," said the king.

Creating An Enduring Business System

"Like Yakubu said, you need to fix your mind on what structure you will eventually grow into. This will grant you the capacity to evolve slowly in a methodical and scientific form. I suppose this is all the value we need to extract from the big grammar of organogram," added the king.

"Now, Yakubu, tell our friends about your 'recipe and prototype,'" requested the king.

"Thank you, my dear king," continued Yakubu.

"I started off during my early business career with one restaurant. Once I could come up with a great meal with some tantalizing taste, I then would find out the ratio of each ingredient that produced such result. This, I called, the recipe; a proportion of each ingredient within the meal. This must be perfected. If the quantity of the meal is doubled for instance, the proportion of ingredient is doubled as well. You can do that only if you can establish the weight of each ingredient. The point of doing this is to make the meal taste the same every time, regardless of where or by whom it is cooked. We need to ensure this for every meal in our menu.

"Beyond the benefit of establishing a sustainable great taste in the head office, this formula gets transferred to all our branches so that if you order a particular meal in one of our outlets in Cape Town, you get the same taste if you take the same meal in Lagos two days later. Coca-Cola tastes the same way, whether you drink it in New York or in Casablanca."

Creating An Enduring Business System

"But Yakubu, I cannot find the relevance of this 'formula-business' to our zoo in India," protested the hunter.

"Thank you so much for that thoughtful observation. If you can get the idea of the recipe as I just explained, you can get the idea of creating a business system just as perfectly," responded Yakubu.

"You need to come up with a way of governance, orderliness and routine administration in that your zoo that is uniquely for your business. A recipe in this sense is a regulated course of action recommended for producing a definite result which can be replicated with precision," continued Yakubu.

"The procedure for employment, individual job description, roles of different heads; all must be well defined and perfected. Every job must be well articulated in a way that your own role as the chairman shall consist essentially of thinking and vision. You become the chief moderator. You conduct regular meetings and do routine checks in order to exercise this function.

"There are two benefits of this: One, the arrangement will ensure that the business continues without you, as you do not need to be there to 'think' and 'see'; it is not mandatory that you conduct meetings everyday. You can indeed, invariably, reduce your job to meeting all those who conduct all the meetings. They let you know what you need to know.

Creating An Enduring Business System

"The other benefit is that this arrangement will permit you to open another zoo elsewhere, starting with some of the established staff members who already know about the business system. They serve as seed employees. New recruits are employed to join them. They coach the new ones; they duplicate, in exact 'copy-form,' precisely the operation in the parent zoo in Delhi. The recipe is to the meal, what the business system is to each branch of the company," concluded Yakubu.

"Oh! That is great. Now what is prototype?" demanded the hunter.

"Yes. Thank you for remembering that," said Yakubu.

"I always call the creation of a business system as coming up with a prototype. The prototype is defined as an original model or pattern from which subsequent copies are made, or improved specimens developed. This original branch you perfect is ancestral to all other branches."

"*Boots Chemist* in England started several years ago with one shop. It now has several branches, which could not have happened if a perfect prototype had not been established within the first shop. In establishing the prototype, no one person, including the owner, should ever be made indispensable. This is vital."

"I can speak of the same truth for the *Mc'Donalds* restaurants you now find almost everywhere, all over the world. Ray Croc bought the first shop from the *Mc'Donalds*

Creating An Enduring Business System

brothers, sustained the recipe per meal, came up with a list of menu per branch, perfected a management system within that little shop that made him needless in the routine duties and then, went on to open another shop and then another shop, until you can now see their restaurants all over the place.

He came up with the basic values, vision, mission statement and ancestral pattern that he went on to replicate on almost every street in all great cities. This is the entire idea of creating a business that thrives in your absence," concluded Yakubu.

"Thank you, Yakubu, for that great stuff," said the king.

"Now, my friends, you can see, you must see why the principle of detachment is ancestral to creating a business system or prototype. You will never have to get in the way of your people as they perform their assigned roles. You will work on your business, rather than work in your business. You become a business owner, rather than a businessman," concluded the king.

The evening session was spent climbing trees, plucking fruits and eating nuts. Everyone claimed to have derived a great benefit from Yakubu's testimony. The zoo manager and the hunter spent the wee hours of the following morning drawing up the organogram and writing the job description for the staff members of the Delhi zoo.

CHAPTER FIVE

Great Ways To Hire Great People

All was set immediately after breakfast for the 'Great ways to hire great people.'
The king thanked Yakubu for the wonderful testimony of vision. He described how impressed he had been with the level of enthusiasm and awareness generated within the duo of zoo manager and his boss.

Yakubu greeted everyone and began.
"Your company, you must remember, is made up of people, not the buildings.

"People problems in management are two-fold; certain people you do have and certain people you don't have. Your greatest headache as a business leader will come from hiring the wrong people. I discovered this truth the hard way.

"Soon after I left the university thirty years ago, I worked with a bank for ten years. I gained some experience and all seemed to be well, except this irresistible desire to create. My dream back in school was to be self-employed as early as I could. I started my first restaurant twenty years ago and got instant goodwill. I felt we needed a new shop in another location to extend our services and to take a greater bite of the market share.

"I hired my best friend. I did that essentially out of share pity. He had been laid off from the same bank I had worked in. He, thereafter, went for job interviews after interviews without luck. He was broke and despondent. He had to put off his proposed marriage for want of cash to care for a new family.

"The fiancée was getting older and his in-laws were nagging. He kept demanding my financial support for his basic needs. The idea of a new shop seemed to come just in time as a perfect solution. I told him of his appointment in the evening and he resumed the next morning. He was to head the existing restaurant with established 'recipe and prototype.' I undertook the task of nursing the new location.

"I can now say, in retrospect, how thoughtless that sympathy decision was. My friend worked with us for eighteen months. It was the most worrisome period of my business career. Trouble was routinized. He brought in strange rules and designed complex policies. He made nonsense of our regulated business system. I had to withdraw two senior managers to my new location as he wanted them dismissed."

"Why didn't you just tell him to go at that stage?"

demanded the hunter.

"I treasured the relationship a great deal," replied Yakubu.

"I figured out that taking such a drastic action would terminate a loving relationship we had nurtured from school. Besides, he had just wedded and the wife was expecting at the time."

"What then happened?" enquired the manager.

"It was horrible, to say the least. Most of the customers stopped coming. He polarized the entire staff. A few saw things his way but majority were unhappy," continued Yakubu.

"Then one day, he told me he was going to start his own restaurant in another part of the city. I could hardly sleep that night. I was extremely excited. He left with a few of my staff the following day. It was after he left and I began to read books on how to hire competent people that I realized how unreasonable my decision was. It also dawned on me, how incompetent I was to have let him stay that long.

"Soon after his departure, one of the senior managers walked up to me, showed me a page on a book that emphasized the wisdom of promoting from within. One of the existing managers would have done a better job of handling the old shop. He would understand the people, the customers, the company culture and the business system.

"The manager fingered a paragraph that spelt the courage I needed during those harsh days. It was a brilliant quote from Abraham Kyper that read: 'When principles that run against your deepest convictions begin to win the day, then battle is your calling, and peace has become sin; you must, at the price of dearest peace, lay your convictions bare before friends and enemies, with all the fire of your faith.'

"We read further and met another invigorating quote from yet another Abraham, this time, Lincoln, who said: 'To sin by silence when they should protest makes cowards out of men!'

"What I want to tell you today is therefore the result of twenty years of practical experience, of reading books on people selection, of monthly retreat to this forest, attending business seminars and putting together an army of the greatest people in many great cities in Africa. It shall, therefore, be a privilege to have your total attention."
Everybody adjusted his sitting position as if fastening their seat belts.

"Your first duty, as soon as there is a vacancy, is to think through the job on paper. Making lists is vital in the job of a businessman," began Yakubu.
"What does this job entail? What are the output responsibilities? When the expected employee resumes and closes everyday; you write down all the various routines

expected of him or her.

"You will also write down all the skills required of an ideal candidate. What is the qualification required by law, if any? Writing all these will help you answer two main questions: 'Can this job be done by one person?' And the other question, 'is there really a vacancy?' You will know that someone going does not always imply a vacancy. Can this job be handled by others simply by sharing the listed responsibilities?

"Writing always lends clarity to your thoughts. It is at the time of writing all these that you fix the interview date and the resumption date. You decide on the training pattern and how soon the employee will be competent.

"The second part of your jotting is to consider the people the candidate will be working with. You ask and answer: 'What kind of attitude and personality will the candidate require?' State all the values required as we mentioned yesterday. The best ability is always dependability. Attitude should carry 90% rating in your requirement consideration, and aptitude, a meagre 10%.

"The third part of your writing is to describe an ideal candidate on paper. This action serves to crystalize your thoughts. The pay-off is always tremendous," concluded Yakubu.

"You talked of fixing a date for interview. Suppose the appointed day arrives and no one shows up?" asked the hunter.

"Yes, that is a funny question," replied Yakubu.

"You will always guard against that," he continued.

"Now that you have exercised this fear, let me run you through the procedure of sourcing candidates for interview.

"As soon as you confirm that there is indeed a space to be filled, start by looking within. Who, among your existing staff, can best fill this position? Promoting someone from within is rated the best source of getting an ideal candidate.

"Your career is a living example of that," commented the hunter.

"Yes, I am a convert of that principle. Experience is always the finest teacher, especially the very bitter ones," continued Yakubu.

"Now, the next best source is an offshoot of the first. This is called personal contact. You ask your existing staff members if they have friends they consider suitable to fill the vacant position. You generate a pool of such in order that you arrange an interview with them.

"I will just itemize the remaining sources without following a particular order," continued Yakubu.

"Depending on the size of your organization, a billboard may be employed in a small to medium sized company, while large corporations may employ the internet, as an avenue of generating candidates for selection.

"There are executive recruiters or placement agencies.

They charge some levies for helping you escape the trouble of a selection process. You may need to put up a newspaper or magazine advertisement. If you do, it may be desirable to show-case your company to represent a picture of an interesting and dynamic organization. You must remember to guard against gender and racial discrimination at all times.

"You may also benefit from a review of the waiting list from your previous interviews. Your customers may also be exposed to the possibility of working with you. You will, therefore, profit from putting your advertisement in your reception, notice boards, websites and all areas where you think they can have easy access to such information," concluded Yakubu.

"Suppose after all these, you still don't get enough candidates?," enquired the zoo manager.

"You will then have to go back to the drawing board," replied Yakubu.

"May be the money you are offering is too low or the advertisement is placed in the wrong channels.

"There is this law of 3 advocated by Brian Tracy; for every position you need to fill, you must generate and interview at least 3 candidates; see them, at least, 3 different times and in, at least, 3 different locations. The importance of this is to ensure that you have reasonable options of candidates to pick from, that you stay as objective as possible by seeing them under different moods and temperaments. You will need to take your time. To hire in a hurry, as I did, is to hire anxiety afterwards. Great haste always grants great waste," concluded Yakubu.

"Now, what do you do on the day of interview?" asked the hunter.

"Thank you for the question," responded Yakubu.

"Before I get to that, I must highlight certain fundamental facts.

First, interviews never come to determine whether a candidate is successful or unsuccessful. The aim is to match the requirement of the job with the attributes and personality of the ideal candidates," stressed Yakubu.

"You mean, to see the company and the vacant position as a beautiful lady, and to determine among all the competing suitors or candidates the one that can represent the ideal life-mate," enquired the king.

"Perfect. Match-making," replied Yakubu.

"The second key highlight is the issue of preparation," continued Yakubu.

"One way is to view yourself as a judge and your panel of interviewers as a jury and that your responsibility is to arrive at a credible verdict. Another way is to see yourself as a doctor and your team as professional colleagues. Your job then is to come up with a life-saving diagnosis. In either case, as interviewers, you will be scientific, methodical and professional in your approach," Yakubu emphasized.

"That can really make one feel very nervous," said the zoo manager.

"A thorough understanding of the procedure will take away all such nerves," replied Yakubu.

"Let me explain a simple format I employ that makes the entire exercise highly exciting, and almost error-free.

"It starts with handling the pool of applicants.

"If the turn-out of candidates is too large, you may have to organize some weeding procedures like conducting some tests on paper or on-line. Such test should have questions that are relevant to the demand of the vacant position. You will therefore reap a short-listed number of candidates that will make the oral interview less cumbersome," concluded Yakubu.

"Yes. You really don't want to sit a panel member to see hundreds of candidates that come in one person after the other," said the zoo manager.

"Exactly," agreed Yakubu.

"And that brings us to the issue of panel members. I always prefer to have between three and seven people on seat. In choosing panel members, I insist on involving the manager or supervisor to whom the new employee will directly report, a team leader or peer (s), who will be working with the new employee and if possible, the human resources (HR) professional. As a rule, I never conduct an interview without having a lady as a member of my panel.

"Ladies, I have confirmed over the years, are human lie-detectors. They are more intuitive than men. With no apparent logical basis, a lady panelist would tell you she felt rather uncomfortable with a particular candidate or that she felt a candidate was hiding something or telling lies. And, in all such situations, they had always been correct. I respect their intuition. In fact, intuition may be the final test in your decision-making criteria," concluded Yakubu.

"Yes. May be ladies are so endowed by the almighty in preparation for their earthly role; they interview suitors all the days of their lives," hinted the king.

There was a roar of laughter, and then, Yakubu continued.

"First, I lay out my entire format on paper well in advance of calling in the first candidate. Next, I do some pep-talk or prayer among the panelists to highlight the importance of the responsibility ahead. Concentration and motivation as weapons of victory are just as priceless in this team of interviewers as in any team that desires to win.

"I then put the file of the first candidate on the table, invite him or her, and the exercise begins.

"I put the candidate at ease, first by calling out the name, then by highlighting the purpose of the interview as essentially match-making. Some of them laugh at this stage. Next, I go ahead to introduce the panel members.

"In court, the order of protocol is to start with the history or substance of the case, the cross examination, the witnesses and evidences and finally, the verdict or judgement. In the hospital consulting room, the doctor takes a quick history, does the physical examination, conducts investigations, long before he arrives at a diagnosis.

"You will do well to follow a similar format. You tell each candidate to give you a brief history about himself or herself; place and date of birth; the parents, the schools attended, childhood experiences, previous employments and all those stuff written on the resume. As he or she begins to talk, the panelists stay attentive. They want to determine the candidate's background, basic values, attitudes and temperaments.

"Questions are then asked to clarify certain issues raised in their talk. Beyond this, I ask him or her: 'Where do you hope to be in five to ten years from now?' This question aims at determining her goal or lack of it, especially whether or not she is ambitious. You will also be able to establish if the position she seeks bears relevance to her future plans," concluded Yakubu.

"They will never be truly happy working with you if your company cannot take them towards their lives main destinations," added the king.

"Yes, that is the idea," agreed Yakubu.

"You take them through their family and social history, as

well as their past achievements. I often ask, 'what is your proudest achievement?' I once asked this question and a lady candidate replied: 'My wedding ceremony.' And as you can imagine, this response provoked uncontrollable laughter among the panel members.

"I always treasure working with intelligent people, especially people I consider smarter than me. Sometimes, to determine this, I ask, 'are you an honest person?'
"No one will ever say 'no' to that sort of question," replied the hunter.
"You are correct," admitted Yakubu.
"Some of them simply link me up with the demand of their religion, and then I ask them the follow-up question: 'Under what circumstances do you tell lies?' At this stage, many of the candidates withdraw into deep thought.

"On one occasion, I met an answer I loved. It was a position for the zonal manager and the candidate was one of our branch managers that had served for ten years. He started by redefining what constituted a 'lie.' 'If a lie means an addition to the truth, as in exaggeration, or a subtraction from the truth, as in understatement, I am sometimes a guilty man.' That to me, sounded very thoughtful and profound. We, however, counter his definition to relieve him of the guilt. I said to him, 'an exaggeration is a truth that has lost its temper, and an understatement, a truth that has gained its modesty.'

"In addition, I demand of them the experience or qualities that qualified them for the job or why, in their own assessment, they considered themselves best suited for the vacant position.

"At other times, I ask: 'Specifically, how do you feel you could contribute?' This cross-examination could go on and on to create vibrant dialogues that could expose hidden attributes, talents and basic values," concluded Yakubu.

"What about the resume or curriculum vitae," asked the zoo manager.

"I will get to that in a minute," replied Yakubu.

"Let me take you through what goes on in my mind while sitting down there listening and staring at the candidate. I call them my thinking tools. There are a series of questions I ask myself in respect of each candidate as they tell their stories and answer the questions.

"I ask myself; 'Will this person be able to work under a harmonious atmosphere in our team?' Ralph Waldow Emerson said: 'Every organization is the lengthened shadow of one man: like manager, like staff members. In using the popular family member model I also ask: 'Will the attitude and personality of this person be in harmony if he were incorporated into my family membership? Does this candidate think like us, talk like us or resemble us as a corporate team? How trainable is this candidate? How teachable?

"We also run each candidate through the SWAN test.

"SWAN is an acronym for Smart, hardwork, ambition and nice, and we expect each candidate to meet these requirements. We never employ people and then go ahead to train them to be nice. We simply employ nice people. People rarely change.

"I also quietly ask and answer, 'can I invite this kind of person, with this sort of personality, to my house for Sunday dinner? If not, why not? Will my people enjoy working with this person?" concluded Yakubu.

"What if the panel members disagree with you on these mental tools," asked the zoo manager.

"Each of them came in through this kind of procedures. They satisfied these criteria. In addition, each of them had been well coached, properly trained on selection procedure long before they were qualified to conduct the interview. If any panel member feels uncomfortable with any particular candidate, we generally don't hire such a candidate," replied Yakubu.

"Yes, but it is already more than a minute that you put off the issue of resume.. I figure that you don't accord it any special relevance," said the zoo manager.

"I will still come to resume. You will profit a great deal from assessing a live candidate, rather than putting emphasis on written information."

There is yet another acid test, SWOT analysis, which we

run each candidate through. SWOT is an acronym for the strength, weakness, opportunity and threat. As you cannot get a perfect spouse, it is unrealistic to demand perfection of any candidate. You will therefore determine the relative strength and weakness. As for opportunity, you want to know if there are hidden talents or capabilities the company can exploit.

"I once interviewed a candidate for an accounting job, only to notice that she exhibited tremendous marketing skills. She was therefore employed on this basis and sent to reinforce the marketing department. Today, she is performing excellently as the Director of Marketing in our corporate headquarters.

"Now, we need to be very careful at the time of interviews. Employing certain candidates may constitute a threat to the entire organization. I have seen many candidates confess their involvement in active unionism in their past employments and how intolerant they had been towards certain corporate policies.

"I have sat and interviewed many candidates who, in the middle of a selection process, began to cry and beg for favourable consideration, some narrated tales of calamities that had befallen them, how desperately they needed the job.

"I was once invited as a panel member representing a multinational company, and one of the candidates threatened to commit suicide if not employed."

"That must be very dangerous indeed," said the hunter.

"Just as a desperate suitor can hide some questionable intentions, you do not want a candidate that will constitute a potential threat to your organization," counseled Yakubu.

"In addition, you will never profit from bringing into your company, a new recruit who is loaded with tales of woe and calamity to share with your team and your customers. As a rule, I developed four main 'don'ts' that help me weed out potential areas of threat.

"One: I don't hire a candidate if I would need to take permission from certain individuals outside my organization before I fire him.

"Two: I don't take 'handout candidates.' Some 'good Samaritans' often arrive and say, 'this fellow needs a job, kindly help fix him up.'

"Three: I don't hire out of sympathy. The experience of my best friend gave me all I needed as a lesson in this regard. I always consider the people the candidate will work with.

Four: This pertains to hiring friends or extended family members. The rule here is simple. If firing such a candidate in the future could carry the potentials of complicating an existing relationship, I always cancel such hiring decisions.

"And as a matter of principle, I never accept an invitation to participate in a panel if any of the candidates is going to interfere with my sense of fairness or objectivity," concluded Yakubu.

"Now, we come to the issue of curriculum vitae or resume," continued Yakubu.

"You must appreciate, at the onset, that most resume are prepared by hired experts and therefore, such documents may not represent a genuine identity or guarantee the credibility of the candidates," said Yakubu.

"I can now see why it is not accorded priority. Why then do people still continue to demand and supply resume?" asked the zoo manager.

"The curriculum vitae has its value. My main area of interest is honesty, credibility and simplicity," replied Yakubu.

"I focus on achievements, not so much the paper credentials. The key is practical accomplishments.

"Has this candidate been jumping from one job to another? Most candidates are generally restless. No sooner have they secured an appointment than you see them attending another interview.

"The last key point is to check the references. Many recruiters would argue that references are generally unhelpful. What I do is to phone them with the attitude of humility, respect and high consideration.

"I dial the number and begin. 'Hello sir. My name is Yakubu. Miss Ann Jacob is applying for a vacant position in our company and has given your name as a referee. Would you be able to spare a few minutes now or can I call you back at another time?

"Generally, most of them tell me to go ahead.

'Could you please tell me some of her strength?' I would demand.

"All you get is an impromptu speech about punctuality, hard work, honesty and commitments.

"When they seemed to have exhausted their points. I ask as a follow-up question: 'To balance up, you know everyone that has areas of strength also keeps certain weaknesses. Can you tell me some of her weaknesses?'

"Some of them at this stage really don't want to talk too much or may even tell you the weaknesses are not noteworthy or significant.

"I then move to the last kicker question: ' Sir, just before I go, is there anything you want me to know about Ann?'

"I then wait quietly. It is at this time that I get the vital information, if any.

"Many expert recruiters also go further and demand to speak to a co-worker or someone else who has worked with the candidate in the past.

"At the end of this individual interview process, my panel would have come very close to making up their minds about a few of the candidates. We then fix another time or date for a group interview," concluded Yakubu.

"Wow! This is very thorough but sounds simple and interesting," said the zoo manager.

"Yes. The candidates themselves enjoy it," replied Yakubu.

"Many corporations these days spend several months interviewing candidates for a few vacant positions. When such employees finally get to work, they take the job very seriously. Besides, they consider themselves winners among several competing candidates and carry such winning attitude to their new assignments.

"You make less mistakes when you take your time than when you do everything in a terrible hurry. My motto is: 'Hire tough, manage with ease," concluded Yakubu.

"Quite sensible," commented the hunter.

"Now, Yakubu, what do you do at the group interview?" asked the zoo manager.

"We call this the Higher Court of Justice," continued Yakubu.

"Justice and fair play are the pillars of a successful selection process. The group interview serves to confirm or validate your on-going decision or verdict in respect of your chosen candidates. Here again, as in all hiring procedures, preparation is the key!

"You organize the panel members as usual. They prepare their minds to pay close attention to each of the candidates and watch their reactions and body chemistry, as you will be seeing all of them together as in a meeting. The operating word here is 'observation.' We invite the surviving candidates and sit them all down in an 'arc' formation around the table.

"The panel leader begins and says something to this effect: 'Good morning ladies and gentlemen. I want to thank you on behalf of our company for your desire to come on board and serve our customers. As you can see, we have seven of you here and there are two vacant positions. We love you all and would ordinarily have preferred to bring all of you in. We are charged with the responsibility of hiring only two candidates, and no more. This is what we want to accomplish this morning. It is one thing for us to label a candidate as suitable, it is another thing for the candidate to consider the job suitable for him or her and then feel comfortable with the position that she wants to get into. This is the reason why our major task today is to tell you about the job and our company, so that you may ask us questions and then make up your minds whether you can carry your interest and intentions further.'

"The moderator, who is generally the panel leader, will then go ahead and tell them a brief history of the company, the mission, values and belief system; the job description, the demand of the job, the company anthem, if any; the hours of duty and possible transfers to other departments or branches. He will tell the candidates about the remuneration patterns, incentives, promotion and people growth within the organization. They will be told about leave periods, probationary periods and uniform, if any. A mention will be made of accommodation, official cars and all that concern the conditions of service.

"The job of the panel members is to check individual reactions as the moderator talks and shifts his gaze from one candidate to another. An ideal candidate will generally agree, nod, get more interested and excited, welcome each of the requirements of the job," continued Yakubu.

"An unsuitable candidate will withdraw, frown, lose interest, look away, disagree, shake her head, or generally show apathy. Some may even show pain as they ask questions about issues of concern in relation to some basic company policies. At the question and answer time, an unsuitable candidate may show 'unconcern' or argue about the premise of some vital company structure or procedures. Some ask questions that invite higher pay and less work.

"The suitable candidates, on the other hand, are seen enjoying themselves; they are happy and excited. They ask lots of intelligent and thought-provoking questions. Some may even come up with questions, ideas and constructive suggestions that make you feel that they already consider themselves happy members of your team.

"My great friends. At the end of the group interview, the panel members can actually tell the most suitable, the runner-up, the third, 4th and so on. The panel members then compare notes, and in all situations, they are almost always in unanimous agreement as to who to pick.

"We often play some little games to confirm our decision. We invite them all in again, tell each of them to write their level of interest in the job at the start of the interview on a scale of zero to hundred. We then collect all the papers. We serve them another set of papers on which they will write their current level of interest, after the interview, again on a scale of zero to hundred. Almost without fail, the suitable candidates commonly reveal improvements in their levels of interest. Some passionate ones say; '100% interested at the onset, now, I think, 1,000%.'

"It is almost impossible to go through all these and err in selection process," said the hunter. "But, I have a question," he continued. "Suppose your best candidate begins to argue with you on remuneration or salary? How do you sort out this kind of thing?"

"That is a great question," began Yakubu.

"First of all, you don't consider an argumentative

candidate as very suitable.

"Next, you don't permit the issue of salary to degenerate into an open negotiation. There is a standard recruitment form in our office which contains the same basic information listed in all resume. In addition, it demands of each candidate to fill in their current pay, and the expected pay. We always have all this information handy before the interview.

"Besides, long before the day of interview, we usually determine what the job is worth in the current market, and we also establish how much we are willing to pay someone in the desired position. If we are hiring someone away from another job, we pay approximately 10% more than his current salary. As a rule, we are always willing to pay well for talented people.

"It is our tradition to start them low and then promise to increase the salary after the 90-days probationary period, based on performance."

"What is probationary period?," asked the hunter.

"A good question. To answer that, you must know that the best of selection procedures cannot guarantee 100% success rate. Like you have trial marriages these days, when some boys and girls choose to live together to establish compatibility, the probationary period is set to determine compatibility between the candidate and the job. Does he love the job? Can he do the job? It is almost a practical component of the interview; an extension of the selection process. They work on the job for 90 days to determine satisfactory performance or otherwise.

"If we consider their performance very satisfactory after this period, we then go ahead and confirm their appointment and fulfill the promised pay rise. There are several instances when the suitable candidate writes an expected salary that is far too low for that cadre. We always stick to our own salary structure, since it is already announced during the group interview," concluded Yakubu.

"I have a silly question," began the hunter. "Suppose a hardworking and diligent husband who has served my company loyally for many years brings his wife for a vacant position in the zoo, what is your take in this respect?," asked the hunter.

"Your question is by no means silly," began Yakubu. "It is very thoughtful and demands the existence or otherwise of a company policy on issues regarding couples working in the same organization. You will need to establish a fixed policy on this. In our business chains, we don't permit such arrangements. We have to develop this approach based on our practical experience. A wife who is loyal at work cannot guarantee a loyal husband in the same establishment. If you dismiss an incompetent husband, you end up dismissing motivation and loyalty in a committed wife and vice versa," concluded Yakubu.

The king ordered a two-hour break. It had been an exciting morning. The hunter felt fully charged and ran into the woods. The parrot, who had been quiet all morning, and his king, flew up the Mahogany tree. Yakubu opened a wooden box containing canned food of all sorts. He started a camp fire and merriment began. The hunter returned from the forest with an armful of fruits, nuts and firewood.

The king kicked the ball rolling for the afternoon session.

"Yakubu, I greatly appreciate the impact of your wonderful testimony on my friends. They can now see that the old ways of doing businesses are obsolete. They are better equipped today to face the challenges of the future and move their zoo into the next level."

"Now that you have talked about the bride; which you claimed to be the job, and the suitor candidate had become the groom, tell my people the best order of protocol immediately after the wedding. They cannot wait to hear what happens on that day when the new employee resumes," concluded the king.

"You ensure two main things at the same time; you start him right, and you start him strong," began Yakubu.

"What do you mean by that," enquired the hunter.

"Let me begin with the first part," Yakubu continued.

"The new employee arrives with a great willingness to start, but carries some low self confidence on the first day.

At this beginning, he needs help. It is required that you introduce him to the job and the other co-workers, as well as the job environment. A familiarization tour or orientation generates a perfect start. You spend a lot of time with him at the beginning. This constitutes 'starting him right.'

"We have a buddy-system: This means the allocation of a capable person that represents a friend to acquaint him with the job and the company. New recruits come loaded with questions and vibrant ideas. They need someone to lean on at this teething stage. They want to discuss the job.

"The other part is to start him up strong. A new employee is eager, willing and ready to get into the new job and get going. He is full of energy. You give him lots of work to do. Work overload makes the job very challenging and highly exciting. He feels valuable to the extent that he feels stretched. This is starting him strong.

"Beyond this, you will accompany work intensity with lots of feedback and discussion. And as soon as possible, you catch him or her doing something right, and if you do, you give praises. You will continue to let your people know how well they are doing. It keeps them motivated and on course," concluded Yakubu.

The hunter thanked Yakubu for helping to expose the hidden secrets of selection process. The king told the group that the theme of the discussion for the next day would be delegation of duties.

CHAPTER SIX

The Amazing Power of Delegation

It was the beginning of another day and all was set for Yakubu to begin.

"I welcome you all to this glorious new day. Our topic today is pivotal," he said.

"I feel happier today more than I have felt since I arrived here. I have grown to know you more and to love you more. Another reason I am very excited is that we are set to discuss my favourite topic; delegation of duties," continued Yakubu.

"I have the time to come here, and the patience to remain here, because one day, I made a decision to learn about delegation. I have read more books, attended more seminars and taught more people about delegation than I have about any other subject. I have practised delegation, and have profited from it, more than I have from any business principle.

"I have put together two great companies in three different continents because of the gains of delegation.

Effective delegation granted me the time and luxury of spending lots of quality moments with my family and friends, while at the same time controlling two giant corporations. Today, I live in Africa, delegation makes it possible. Tomorrow, I may choose to live in New Delhi, London, New York or China. Delegation will grant this freedom.

"Your job is to sit, relax, listen and take notes as you will hear the finest practical ideas on business handover; ideas that are usable and profitable. You need such ideas that will finally set you free, that will pronounce you discharged and acquitted from a self-imposed prison sentence of a tiring business place.

"My great king. Today, they will be spared all the voluminous theories and lousy jargons. What they are about to hear, they will never get in any one book. It is a synthesis of several years of study and application and of acquiring the knowledge and wisdom of thousands of great thinkers," Yakubu promised enthusiastically.

"I really cannot wait. Start right away," interrupted the hunter.

"Then, if you are ready, let us begin with a long list of 'important reasons' why people don't delegate," said Yakubu.

"First, people do not know that delegation carry such a great benefit. They do not have the motive. They, therefore, take no time to learn how to delegate.

"Next, many people think there is no time to teach others on how to do the job well. It seems quicker and reasonable to do the task themselves rather than teach and correct the mistakes.

"Another excuse is the erroneous belief that subordinates are incompetent of handling complex duties. Other people don't delegate principally because they consider themselves renown experts and then feel that nobody is good enough on the job. A few other managers brush aside the practice of delegation because they want to feel on top of their jobs.

"I have several friends we started off together who still work in the same old shop of twenty years because, according to them, they love cooking and therefore consider it unwise or difficult to drop something they genuinely love doing. They are therefore stuck in the kitchen.

"My best friend I told you about nurtures his own peculiar excuse. His people are simply not trustworthy. He once told me that he had a terrible dream one night. In the dream, one of his supervisors branched off from him, opened his shop right opposite his restaurant, went away with all his staff members and customers and left him completely stranded. He claimed he was extremely angry with this development in that scary dream.

"He did not know what went over him. His anger was

uncontrollable. Suddenly, he went for a gun, ran across the street to the supervisor's new shop and shot him in the chest. He was contemplating feeding his meat to the vultures when the police arrived. He was instantly arrested and several violent blows were rapidly delivered on his forehead. He wasn't particularly sure of the final punch that made him fully awake but he met himself on the bed, panting and deeply wet with cold sweat.

"He claimed to be so wet that his loving wife, who was arriving early that morning from her parents, couldn't believe that he hadn't urinated on himself. He, thereafter, vowed never to reveal the secret of his business to any of his staff members. That was the terrible case of my best friend," concluded Yakubu.

"Yes, most of our suspicion of others are aroused by what we know about ourselves, nothing so completely baffles one who is full of tricks and duplicity himself, than straight forward and simple integrity in another," said the hunter.

"Thank you my wise friend," continued Yakubu.

"Trust is the foundation of any relationship; social or business. When you trust men, they will be true to you; if you treat them greatly, they will show themselves great. The people we trust naturally tend to be trustworthy. He who mistrusts most must be trusted least. Your job is, therefore; to always find a way to hire honest and credible people.

The Amazing Power Of Delegation

You review and perfect the skill of hiring great people. And once you put them on the job, you put a control system in your business system. You never really throw caution to the winds. It is equal foolishness to trust everybody, and to trust nobody.

"Finally, as we continue, the vast majority of people do not delegate because they do not know how," Yakubu revealed.

"Thank you very much, Yakubu," said the appreciative hunter.

"I think we already have sufficient reasons why many people do not delegate. Even though you never mentioned my name, it was clear that I was included in the very first group and the very last group of people. I didn't know it was very profitable to delegate and I didn't know how to do it. Now that I know it is the key to further growth, just go ahead right away and tell me how," demanded the hunter.

"There are certain basic foundations I must address before we get going. It is always necessary to clear the field and dig the ground long before we sow the seed," began Yakubu.

"You must know that I will be putting together the basic requirement for assigning a single task, of delegating complex responsibilities, as well as the demand of handing over an entire business empire," continued Yakubu.

"If your goal is to ultimately hand over an entire

business to your subordinate or children, you must perfect the skill of saving. If you can learn to drive, type, cook or walk, you can learn to save. Saving is an art that deserves proper learning and practise. I recommend you read **'The Greatest And Strangest Money Making Secrets,'** written by Dr. Abib Olamitoye, which can serve as your companion in this respect."

"What has saving got to do with handing over a business concern?" enquired the hunter.

"You need a growing financial reserve. This will grant you tolerance and some feeling of security. You need money to cushion the cost of mistakes the apprentice on delegation will incur. The more money you have, the less you fear that his error may prove fatal. You feel relaxed and reassured.

"Next, you will profit from a calm temper. This will permit the delegatee to see your love for her and her ultimate growth, rather than your rigid attachment to the task and the anticipated success of the business. Your goal must always be to use the business to grow the people, rather than to use the people to grow the business.

"You start by setting goals for a workplace on auto-pilot. You describe on paper, the whole picture of the desired outlook, when the business is being run entirely by your people.

"As to the transfer of your business to your children, the basic rule is your willingness and ability to prepare such children for the business, rather than the all too familiar task of preparing the business for the children.

"You must know that leaders who develop people add, while leaders who develop leaders multiply. Your job at the onset shall, therefore, consist of finding one person, teaching that single person all you know about the demands of the job, and making him or her a superstar. You make the person a leader.

"I am aware that you have been coached on the principle of detachment. The idea of dying-while-alive is priceless, if you are to delegate without pain. Delegation is an exercise in selling. You are transferring feelings. You are handing over the love, passion and enthusiasm you have for the work to the delegatee. They catch your fever. You will need to learn how to sell well.

"How can your people want to do what you want them to do? There must be some benefit in it for them. How much do you know about people and the things that move them to act? You will therefore profit from what you have learnt on people skills.

"Now, like most of my friends, if you ever find yourself unduly in love with a routinized task, of getting inseparable from certain pleasant procedures, you must recognize that such procedure is the greatest enemy of your advancement. This is the only enemy you will never be permitted to forgive. You will, therefore, design a strategy that can promise its ultimate death. A simple approach is to develop a new found love in the process of teaching such a pleasure-giving task to a subordinate, until he becomes proficient. You are therefore liberated to face a fresh and higher assignment that can bring superior results. This new assignment, once perfected, will in turn be delegated, so that you may face a higher role and secure a better position. This is the only way you can grow and ascend as a leader.

"The man who gets the most satisfactory results is not always the man with the most brilliant single mind, but rather, the man who can best coordinate the brains and talents of his associates. If you always struggle to do what others can do, then you are liable to leave undone, what only you can do. Further growth is therefore impeded.

"Now, you can see, you must see that delegation is the basic skill needed to maximize your full potentials; to make your full contribution and earn more; to grow as fast and as far as you possibly can. Your willingness and ability to delegate effectively can accelerate your career more than any given factor. It remains the critical constraint on your capacity to grow in value as a leader.

"Delegation is a form of giving. You must have heard it said that: 'The more you give, the more you get.' As you share responsibility and authority, you indirectly generate higher responsibility and assume greater authority. Delegation is people empowerment. You become more powerful as you empower others.

"Before I go to the procedure of delegation, let me stress two key issues. You will need to have confidence in the delegatee's ability. All you have mastered today, someone taught you. You gained mastery because your teacher trusted your ability.

"Finally, you need to remember the importance of creating a back-up star as you develop, grow and shine a superstar within your establishment. This is called 'a successor' or simply, 'a deputy' concluded Yakubu.

"What do you think is the way out for that your best friend who is scared of delegation and who is suspicious of his employees. How can he get away from distrust and suspicion?," asked the zoo manager.

"I don't suppose you want to act like him?" asked Yakubu.

"You must not bite the finger that feeds you," advised Yakubu.
"If you open a zoo very close to that of your boss, if you deliberately cart away a portion of his customers and operate within his circle of influence, you do yourself a great disservice on the long run.

"You can see this great Mahogany tree that carries the empire of the loving king. If a little Mahogany seed begins to sprout underneath its shades, the manure generated by the fallen leaf may make it appear to grow rapidly at the onset, but soon, the supply for more nutrients will be cut short. First, the big Mahogany already has established roots which are hard to compete with, so, the roots of the young plant can only access superficial and scanty nutrients."

"Next, the shade of the big Mahogany tree will disallow any form of sunshine which the new shoot will need for food preparation. It will therefore have a stunted growth.

"Your boss, the hunter, already knows certain business principles about which you are ignorant. He is far ahead of you in information, infrastructure, business structure, savings and other management skills. He has more competitive advantage.

"The hunter will have more time to learn fresh ideas were you to get away from him today and compete with him. His income will therefore accelerate faster than yours. We are in a world where the winner takes all, while the rest make do with the crumbs. You need to find a location where you can become a big fish in a small pond, rather than a small fish in a big pond. This is the entire idea.

"You will need your boss during your teething stage of commencing business. He can only be more forthcoming as a mentor if you are not seen as competing with him. Just one timely advice from this experienced hunter can save you thousands of dollars and needless labour in a foolish and vain attempt to figure things out using mere innate intelligence," concluded Yakubu.

"I thank you very much for your warning," replied the zoo manager.

Then he continued, facing Yakubu.
"I have it all written in my note. One day, I may be privileged to teach it to others. Loyalty is an important family value drummed into me while growing up.

"My boss' confidence in me has brought me this far. I consider it an exercise in true love and great trust. I see him as loving me more than he does the zoo. If I leave him tomorrow and capture his customers, that will be, proclaiming that I treasure his customers' money more than the idea of earning the respect of he that loves and respects me. This, to me, is the entire story and essence of true loyalty," continued the zoo manager.

"Your good friend was at the brink of disaster and humiliation. You were there as a friend in need. You invited him to eat and he worked really hard to slow down or stop the pace of your own cutlery. I think I recognize his situation today more than anyone here. I do not wish to be in his kind of shoe at any stage of my career. There are thousands of virgin territories for me to delve into when the time arrives.

"Today, your friend may be facing some guilt feelings that could interfere with his inner peace. Such peace is needed for progress. Guilt feelings make people think of, and expect nemesis. And sure enough, that is what they get.

Fear and suspicion that his own subordinates might pay him back cannot make him consider the gains of delegation. He, therefore, develops an inescapable iron bar that curtails his ascent," he concluded.

"The zoo manager is well meaning and right thinking," commented the parrot.

"You can see from his calm response that he is very wise indeed. To profit from good advice naturally requires more wisdom than to give it. We were together in the zoo in the last twelve months. He is clever, straightforward, diligent and considerate. He operated the zoo as if it belonged to him, especially in the absence of his boss.

"Yakubu, I suggest you go ahead and describe the process of delegation to my good friends; you really need to be brief, for it is with words as with sunbeams; the more they are condensed, the deeper they burn," said the parrot.

"Thank you, the deputy king," continued Yakubu.

"Permit me to answer the zoo manager's questions. No one individual can really help another unless and until such a needy person is ready. Like they say, ' when the student is ready, the teacher will appear.'

"I am confident that my best friend will one day outgrow his current limitations and circumstances. If he ever nursed any guilt like you guessed, advance wisdom will teach him to forgive himself and release the pains. I have long forgiven him. I have been more than compensated for the good turn I did to him. I pray for him and wish him well. This is the very best I think I can do to help," continued Yakubu.

"And now, back to our discussion, your main duty as a business leader is to get the highest return on your company's investment in people. One of the greatest talents of all is the talent to recognize and develop talent in others. Your job is to grow people, and only people can grow. All the other assets like the computers, furniture, machinery and vehicles depreciate. People appreciate. You employ delegation to bring out the best in your people.

"The starting point of every effective delegation is to think through the job on paper. You write down in details the full description of the job. You then go ahead to illustrate how it will be like when the job is perfectly accomplished. This latter description is called standard of performance. It is like the control experiment in the laboratory. The third step is to determine a schedule for getting the job done. You ask and answer, how long will it take to get this job done?

"The point here is to assign a single task successfully until mastery is attained and sustained. You employ the same procedure to bring in another task, then another task, until mastery is achieved. This way a complex task is delegated.

"There are three main categories of new employees. The fresh ones who lack basic knowledge of the new job, the medium, who have a fair idea or some form of experience, and the third, the experts, the professionals.

"You use different approaches of delegation in each of these three classifications.

For the green recruits, you use the directive style of delegation. You say: 'Watch me as I do it. You will do the next.'

"For the people with some form of experience on the job, you set clear goals, the standard of performance and then you come up with a deadline. You direct your delegatees to get going with the job. Your clear message to them is to come back to you only when they are stuck, when they run into a problem. This is called management by exception. They keep going except when they hit obstacles.

"As for the pros. You use easy interaction as a method of delegation. Your role here is that of a counselor, mentor or a guide.

"There are a few other points to note about delegation. We have mentioned that the first law of management is to pick the right person. This means, matching the requirement of the job to the ability and personality of the person. There are four main personality types. Each personality type requires a different approach to delegation in order to maximize effectiveness.

"The first type is the relater. They tend to be sensitive and indecisive. They are people-oriented and score low in task orientation. They treasure getting along with others, cooperation, friendliness, harmony and team spirit. You will have to determine who, among your staff members fits this category. In delegating to such a person, your approach shall be low-key, you will be concerned with feelings and show warmth, caring and friendliness.

"The second personality type is the thinker. These people score low in people or task orientation. They are very concerned about details, accuracy, precision, in being correct and thorough. Again you find out if your delegatee fits this category. In delegating to the thinkers you will have to be specific. You get to the point and emphasize the details, accuracy and precision.

"The director is the third personality type. They are more tasks focused but low in people orientation. Directors are more concerned with getting results. They are achievement driven and impatient; they decide quickly and tend to be in a hurry. Again, you determine any of your staff members who fits this category. Your approach to delegation here is to specify very clearly the required result and the ways such results and achievements will be measured.

"The last personality type is the expressive or the socialite. They are very friendly, enthusiastic and outgoing. They see only the big picture and are very impatient with details. They are all over the place. You determine who among your staff members fits this expressive category.

The Amazing Power Of Delegation

Your job in delegation shall consist of keeping him on track and to focus his energies where he can make the greatest contribution. You can then get others to perform tasks that require details.

"Like I said earlier, you delegate limited, smaller tasks to build courage and confidence. You end up delegating the entire job. The more responsibility you grant your people, the stronger they become," concluded Yakubu.

"Please, shine some light on the idea of handing over my zoo to my son," demanded the hunter.

"You employ the same technique. You start by writing out a comprehensive list of what you do as a chief executive officer in the zoo, leaving nothing out. Then, starting from the simplest, you assign the first task until mastery is sustained. You bring the next and the next until the entire task is taken over. The ideal approach is however, to let him start at the bottom like everyone else.

"If he is to end up presiding over a team of managers, it makes sense if he has been one of the managers for a while. To become a manager, he should have merited such position on account of superior performance as a supervisor. All such arrangement will work well to the degree that he starts at a lower level as an employee, and the more you make him buy the basic values and working principles of the zoo.

"When delegating, you need to state the outcome in

clear terms and make such measurable. You delegate with participation and discussion. You explain the how, what, why and when of the task. The more an employee gets to talk and dialogue about the job, the more he understands it, accepts it, loves it and ultimately stays committed to it," Yakubu explained.

"You let them know the resources that will be available to them. Will doing this job require that they are permitted the involvement of certain other staff members, the use of computers, company vehicles, offices and all such facilities? The grand mission of delegation would have been accomplished when the delegatee walks away feeling: 'This is my job,' concluded Yakubu.

"How much responsibility can we permit on a scale of one to hundred? Yakubu, I am worried about mistakes," asked the hunter.
"Thank your for that great question," replied Yakubu.
"You end up giving 100% responsibility. Giving 100% responsibility is a great motivator of maximum involvement and of superior performance. Your destination as delegators, upon arrival, is the surrender of every component of the task. You must remember, though, that you are still accountable for the result. Your people are essentially an extension of your hands," responded Yakubu.

"I should keep eternal vigilance?," demanded the

hunter.

"I won't call it that," answered Yakubu.

"Your job is to surrender more in order to free your hands for higher assignments. You conduct regular supervision. Once your delegatees are fully taught on how to do the job well and they have achieved some level of competence, let them know that you have complete trust in them, that you have confidence in them. Tell them so. This raises their self esteem. It makes them feel confident. To feel confident is to feel competent. Expressing confident expectation is priceless in people building. They seldom disappoint your expectation," Yakubu counseled.

"The psychology of expectation is of inordinate importance. Permit me to mention two main effects of expectation. The first called the Pygmalion effect, states that people perform in ways that are consistent with the expectation they have picked up from their leader, both consciously or unconsciously.

The second, by far the most powerful, the Galatea effect, is the employee's opinion of his ability and his self-expectation about his performance. If a person thinks he can succeed, he will. The Pygmalion effect can influence the Galatea effect. The leader can reinforce self belief in the subordinate.

"Suppose they come back to demand your involvement?" asked the zoo manager.

"Excellent question," remarked Yakubu.

"Every job can be divided into series of steps. The person who has the next step owns the job. When they come back to you to do a bit of the task, like helping out to check some information, data, or to source for some manual, you tell them where to get such information.

"You must refuse to take back what you have assigned. You do that when you over-supervise or when you put further progress on hold by promising to help talk to an officer about the task, or help source for internet information. All you are doing is encouraging upward delegation. Let them go ahead and do every component of the job," concluded Yakubu.

"So when they ask for help, we tell them to help themselves," enquired the zoo manager.

"That is the point," agreed Yakubu.

"I can assure you that some delegatees will keep coming at every stage as they encounter new challenges or unanticipated obstacles. If we must help with every problem, then we hinder their capacity to make decisions and solve problems.

"So what do we do when they are stuck?" asked the hunter.

"Great," remarked Yakubu.

"There is a form in our office for this purpose. Basically, it consists of dotted lines that demand the definition of the problem, the causes of the problem, all the possible solutions to the problem and lastly, the best solution. Everyone coming up with a difficult problem is required to begin by spending some time filling out the form.

"The rule is simple. Fill out the form, figure out the best solution and apply the solution. They can then go to the superior officer or delegator only if the problem persists in spite of their best efforts," Yakubu explained.

"With arrangements like this, people are forced to think. When they do, they stand a greater chance of coming up with the correct solution," admitted the hunter.

"Yes. This will make your staff members grow in their capacity to think, decide and solve problems," said Yakubu.

"That is great. People become smarter, stronger and more valuable," added the zoo manager.

"When thinking, decision-making and problem-solving are routinized in your establishment; you can travel for months and your people will keep the flag flying. The business will literally thrive in your absence," commented the king.

"Now, how do you ensure they actually perform the task to the right standard, that they produce excellent performance?" demanded the hunter.

"Perfect question," began Yakubu.

"This is always the purpose of superior supervision. It always serves a good end if you establish what quality results look like and ensure that they meet such standard."

"A great approach is always to apply the factory model of productivity to your people, your various departments and branches. In every factory, there are inputs of funds, time, supplies, machinery and training. Within the factory, there are various activities; the conveyor belts, the processing, the machines and the labeling. Now, out of the factory, there are outputs or results of the process. To get excellent results, your main attention must center on the outputs. How can you increase the quality and quantity of the output? How can we make the most of the human resources?

"The key fact about generating quality products is all about incremental improvement. It is all about a relentless pursuit of excellence, what the Japanese call Kaizen. Business is dynamic. You must keep improving the quantity and quality all the time.

"A valuable tool is to keep improving the people who invariably produce the expected result. You determine the key result areas for every staff member. Why are the people on the pay roll? What specifically are they required to accomplish? What can each staff member do, that if done well, will generate valuable contribution?

"All excellent managers always strive to bring the very best out of their people. They make the key result area written, measurable and time bounded," concluded

The Amazing Power Of Delegation

Yakubu.

"I am a convert of Yakubu's approach," said the king. "Your chief responsibility is to teach the people how the job is to be done. All managers are teachers. As soon as you have mastered a set of skills, teach your subordinates and then move on to learn and then master higher and greater skills. This is the only way you are permitted to grow a great empire," concluded the king.

"That is a powerful testimony," commented the hunter.

"Before we conclude our discussion, permit me to leave you with this final note," began Yakubu.

"You must remember to always inspect what you have assigned. This conveys to the subordinate that the job is important. You are not getting rid of the assignment. You are still held accountable for the result and performance of your people.

"Tomorrow, we shall be looking at what to do if you encounter a staff member that cannot do the job well. You, sometimes, do encounter some incompetent employees, regardless of the finest approach at hiring the best people."

Everyone left on a happy note.

CHAPTER SEVEN
Firing Incompetent People

It was to be the last day of sharing testimony. All was set, and Yakubu was told to begin.

"Today is the last day of the series of testimony in this woods. I want to take the next hour telling you a perennial issue in business management."

"You are such a great and benevolent man," the hunter remarked.

"You deserve to be celebrated and decorated for your immense contributions to people enrichment and business development, not only in Africa, but everywhere on the planet earth.

"You wear so much innocent look and parade such simplicity that no one would ever reckon that you carry this much business awareness, and this much light. You have helped to rekindle my ailing spirit and to rediscover my lost hope. I will reproduce this forest testimony so that unborn generations of Asians will be grateful that I came this far. You have been a great blessing to us here as your career has represented generosity and benevolence among your people, your very fortunate people.

"Yakubu. I cannot thank you enough. Certainly, God can; He shall," said the hunter.

"I thank you, the great hunter, for your kind words," responded Yakubu, as he continued.

"Your willingness to know, your desire to grow, has produced what you have received. To have travelled this far in search of knowledge is commendable. Only the very best in any calling will carry this level of will; a passionate will to win, and a vigorous will to prepare to win. Your minds carry so much fertility that any viable seed of practical knowledge will sprout and blossom and bear great harvest.

"My dear friend. I urge you to keep your will alive; keep your hope alive. You have come this far not so much to learn how to share testimonies, but that your life may henceforth be a visible testimony. You can preach a greater sermon with your life than with your lips. With this level of will, nothing can stop your accelerated climb to a position of prominence. I truly wish you the very best.

"Today, we shall discuss about the skill of letting the incompetent people go, so that the competent ones can have some breathing space. Let me start by reminding you again of the woeful business decision I made at the start of my restaurant. I am talking about the decision to hire my best friend. My friend knew he was not suited for the job. I knew. Everyone knew. Now came the other woeful decision or indecision; I let him stay.

"Each time I rested my thought on his activities within the restaurant, I felt some deep pain. I didn't know what to do. I needed some courage. I knew the solution was to let him go but he wouldn't go. Since I did the hiring, I knew it was my responsibility to do the firing.

"I associated more pain to firing him than to letting him continue. That was why I told you that the happiest day in my early business career was that glorious morning when he announced that he was leaving.

"When I began reading books on effective ways to manage business. I spent hours reading again and again, how best to let incompetent people go. It is important that you learn, practise and master some stress-free techniques of getting rid of unsuitable employees. If you cannot fire the incompetent employees, you cannot hire the competent ones either.

"Business is like respiration. You breathe by taking in the great people and then letting out the incompetent ones. Your duty in business is to keep breathing and to breathe properly. If you stop breathing in this sense; either by neglecting to rid the business place of incompetent people or avoid taking in the competent ones, then business death invariably becomes inevitable. There are great ways to breathe with ease. In the coin of business, hiring is head and firing is tail," Yakubu pointed out.

Firing Incompetent People

"I love your metaphor. You are getting me fired up," interrupted the hunter.

"We live in a moment of history where change is so speeded up that we begin to see the present only when it is already disappearing. Change is accelerating. Let me start by giving you some basic statistical facts. First, business is dynamic. Competencies required for effectiveness in the past are now obsolete. To stay relevant in the business arena, employees must improve. Some don't or wont," continued Yakubu.

"Statistical findings reveal that about 30% of employees don't work out, and 70% of these incompetent ones expect you to do the job of letting them go. They want to leave but are not competent enough to take the necessary action. They need your help."

"We do them a great service by showing them the way out?" enquired the zoo manager.

"Exactly," continued Yakubu.

"One of the most unkind things you can do is to keep a person in a job for which he or she is not appropriate," he added.

"It can be very frustrating," agreed the zoo manager.

"The person who keeps an incompetent employee, demonstrates greater incompetence than such an employee," Yakubu continued.

"Nothing sabotages your future more than keeping an

incompetent person. We are told that 80% of the troubles in the workplace are caused by 20% of the people. Your job as a business leader is to figure out the 20% of the people before they cause the dreaded trouble. Troubles, like weeds, thrive on lack of attention. Prevention, is said, to be cheaper than cure. One way of keeping this eternal vigilance is to employ the zero based thinking."

"What is zero based thinking?" enquired the hunter.

"The zero based thinking used in this sense helps to question the employability of each of your employee, on a regular basis. It is a mental tool, a thinking skill that permits you to demand of yourself, as a business manager, in respect of each of your employees, this question: 'Knowing what I now know about this person, would I go ahead to hire him or her if I have to do it all over?'

"Suppose the answer is no, you wouldn't?" asked the zoo manager.

"Then your next question becomes: 'How do I remove this person, and how fast?,'" answered Yakubu.

"Imagine you see one rotten apple in a basket full of healthy apples. When will you get it out? What is the danger of putting off the decision to remove it?

"Your job is to employ the zero based thinking all the time. You are most free from danger, even when safe, you are on your guard. A danger foreseen is half avoided.

"Some very bitter experiences and hours of study have

taught me this policy: Hire slowly, and if need be, dehire quickly. The opposite is unprofessional. You regret at leisure if you hire quickly and dehire slowly. I cannot teach you a kinder approach. As soon as the young employee begins the ninety-day probation period, you do as much as you can to ensure his success at the job. If you discover any irredeemable mismatch, you let the person go as quickly as possible," stressed Yakubu.

"Yes. I agree with you totally," said the hunter.

"If one goes ahead to confirm an appointment following an unsatisfactory performance in the course of the ninety days probation, the employee will begin to consider the job as a permanent duty, and he begins to rely on the income. If you now fire at some late period, it becomes cruel and quarrelsome," concluded the hunter.

"That is a considerate and thoughtful comment," Yakubu admitted.

"Now, Yakubu, how do you determine true incompetence in an employee? I mean, how do you tell 'won't do' from 'can't do'?" asked the hunter.

"That is an excellent question," began Yakubu.

"There is a simple test we adopt. You ask and answer in respect of the troubled employee; could this person do this job well if their life depended on it? if the answer is yes, they could do it, then we are dealing with motivation problem. And if no, they couldn't do it if their life was at stake, then we are dealing with a case of true incompetence," explained Yakubu.

Then he went on, "fully 80% of problems with employees are company created. In most companies, we have lack of direction, timely feedback, recognition, praise and reward system.

"All these melt down to poor commitment and de-motivation. You wouldn't expect an excellent performance from an employee, for instance, who is doing his best in an inappropriate role.

"Dehiring after confirmation of appointment should only come from unrepentant attitudinal flaws, serious misconducts or gross incompetence. The approach to dehiring, in whichever case, is essentially the same.

"Before you attempt to resolve any performance problem, you must do your homework thoroughly.

"You come up with adequate documentation and then get the facts of the problem. You must know that many people are doing their jobs and are not aware that their performance is unsatisfactory. Your immediate aim is to save the employee.

"The professional approach is to start off with a review of the employment contract or a letter explaining what the person's job is. Then you invite the employee. Always have someone with you when a performance discussion takes place so that you have both a witness and a calming influence. Next, you document the discussion with a memo, which is subsequently filed away in the employee's record.

"Like you were told on people skill, you never use any destructive criticism. You blame the act and not the person. In the end, you mention relieving phrases like 'next time something like this happens, I expect you to do ... ",
in the future, I expect you to do this ...; or, why don't you try it this way?"

"What I do is simple. Long before a decision to let-go is contemplated, I invite the person, state the facts of the case and request possible corrective measures. In most cases, the person is remorseful and we wind up with a promise of improvement. I make a written agreement on the nature of improvement and the key issues discussed and keep such in his file. I actually make him or her sign such an agreement.

"Your primary goal is to correct performance problems; you accomplish this when you can positively influence future behaviour and build sustainable motivation for continued improvement for both the employee and the team.

"I usually repeat this process, often, with a different offence, for the same employee, until the employee's attitude and competence improve, or until dismissal becomes inevitable. The basic rule is one, two, three and out," concluded Yakubu.

"That is great. Now, what does one do on the day of dismissal," demanded the zoo manager.

"You start with preparation. You review the file, all your previous meetings," began Yakubu.

"Next, you make up your mind about the severance package. This is a cash gift that acts as a bridge to help the person make a painless transition to a new job.

You need to bear in mind that people generally don't change. You should, therefore, resolve to do what must be done. The ideal venue for dismissal is a separate office or a meeting room, away from your office. Afterwards, you want to be able to get up and leave. You cannot leave if it were conducted in your office. Again, you should have a witness present.

"The best time to let a person go is early in the week. The next morning, they can start job searching. You need to be firm and unemotional. No anger. You must remember that inability to do a job does not mean that the person is bad. You never reiterate the mistake that they have made. The chief aim is to protect the self esteem of the person at all cost. Therefore, you'll be kind, calm and compassionate.

"You say something like this: 'I have given this matter a lot of thoughts, and I feel strongly that there is no compatibility between you and this job. I am sure you'll be happier and more fulfilled working in a different setting,'" Yakubu stated.

"What if they keep arguing and resisting?" asked the hunter.
"You just keep affirming: 'I really believe you'll be happier in a new environment.'
You repeat it calmly and firmly over and over again until he stops arguing and finally accepts.

"And once he has accepted, you simply explain the resources that are available to him. You may agree on a face-saving cover story and then, you stick to the story.
You avoid giving fake promises or raising false hopes. Sometimes, I tell them to simply resign, and some do," said Yakubu.

"Suppose they become disagreeable and threaten legal actions?" asked the hunter.
"Yes, you may need to seek legal advice on appropriate ways to dehire in certain complicated cases," replied Yakubu.

"You will agree that if you start off hiring nice people, if the foundation of your interview is rooted in getting people with great attitude, rather than emphasize on great aptitude, then you reduce the chances of complications and litigation, if and when you, indeed, need to let people go. Such 'nice people' simply go away without acrimony, especially when you dehire with fairness and compassion. They believe you, and trust your judgement. They march on with a perception that the two parties could need each other's references; that you could meet again under a different setting and still be friends.

"You must know that no one case is exactly the same as the other. You will, therefore, learn from experience, and exercise gentleness and compassion at all times. When you do become proficient in breathing in and breathing out in this business sense, you'll get your business career completely transformed," concluded Yakubu.

"I thank you, Yakubu. It has all together been greatly insightful," said the king.

Everyone was delighted with the entire experience of the forest retreat. With a great mission now accomplished, the return trip to India was planned for the early hour of the next morning. For the moment, the colony began a send-forth party that went deep into the night. There was an air of excitement, empowerment, resolution and determination all the way back to the continent of Asia. They both seemed to say: "Hats off to the past; sleeves up for the future."

CHAPTER EIGHT

Conclusion

Fortunately, this fascinating story had a profoundly happy ending. The hunter returned to India, converted the forest teaching into a practical check-list and went ahead to progressively build his zoo into a famous company. He delegated everything except thinking; empowered his team, worked on his zoo, rather than in his zoo; he began other businesses and grew them into a towering conglomerate. He became one of the wealthiest men of his generation. He made more money and fame, generated more fulfillment and freedom and touched more lives than he would have ever dreamed possible. He visited the forest regularly and became a life-long friend of the rich Yakubu and the kingdom of Parrots.

The hunter made the check-list his lifetime companion and kept reliving Yakubu's testimonies and the thrilling experiencees in the forest gathering. His business did not only thrive in his absence, he went ahead to create valuable time for social activities, charity programmes, family

Conclusion

holidays and some regular quiet retreats for inner growth and serenity.

Here is, perhaps, the most inspiring bit. The hunter narrated the exciting story of his ambitious adventure to his children. They got encouraged. He taught them the great principles behind Yakubu's stunning testimonies. The children perfected the skills and thereafter took over the management of the Delhi zoo and other thriving businesses while the hunter was still young and strong. They infused vibrant ideas and youthful passion into the businesses. The hunter stepped back and watched with keen interest and deep satisfaction as his business empire prospered and multiplied right to his ripe old age.

The zoo manager later relocated to Mumbai, another great and promising city in India, started his own business and became fabulously wealthy. He compiled Yakubu's incredible testimonies, the king's immortal laws and the sterling principles of detachment into a business manual and then came up with a miracle book, "How To Create A Business That Thrives In Your Absence." The book caught the attention and admiration of several great minds and zealous entrepreneurs and subsequently, became a classic tool for people enrichment and business development.

Book By The Authour

Praise For The Book

I must commend you after reading your book on the above title.

I received 3 copies of the book on behalf of my organization and decided to go through one. I was able to finish it within a day and will still read it again. It is the best book and most inspiring I'v ever read. I wish I'v seen this book 5 years ago.

My people used to say that when a wound heals, you'll forget that it was once painful. I am really proud of you to have come from such a background to make fortunes, and have learnt among other things that one should not complain; that hardwork does not kill and that giving is not only important but a way out of poverty.

It amazes me how you are able/willing to share the secrets of your success, which many Nigerians who have made it are not willing to disclose for fear of competitions and selfishness.

Keep up the good work. God is watching.

-Enyinna Uneke ENYI. *Executive Assistant, Administration. Afribank Plc.*

Your book, which you recently delivered to my office, is the most fascinating book I have read in recent times. I must confess, when I saw it on my desk two days ago, I just shoved it aside. "Who is interested in making money?" I asked. But in my spare moment this morning. I decided to read one or two pages. You won't believe me that I have not put it aside since then! I have read 80%. It is beautifully written in simple English and the delivery is impressive and captivating! Honestly, you have A BIG SELLER IN YOUR HANDS. YOUR GOLDEN BOOK MUST BE CELEBRATED!

- B.G.K. Ajayi. *President, Ibadan College of Medicine Alumni Association Worldwide.*

'Unputdownable!' That is the description that best fits Dr. Olamitoye's work; a work that combines the commonsense of modern money management with the timeless wisdom of ancient philosophies of life.

Going through the work reveals an author who is not only well versed in entrepreneurial experience, but who has learnt and benefitted immensely from the secret teachings of ancient masters on the issues of wealth, well being and health management.

The wealth of the book's content must have informed the decision of the Tribune management to endorse the book for its teeming prospective readers. The style is appealing and lucid and the language is near-perfect.

- Lanre Oyetade. *Group Business Editor and Co-ordinator of Personal Finance Series for the Nigerian Tribune Newspaper*

Cat No 001 CD

Easy approach to successful advertising for the small business owners. Oiling the wheels of sales

Cat No 002 CD

The Amazing Power Of Team Building. How to unleash synergy and creative potentials

Cat No 003 CD

The two reasons why business is created plus powerful tools to revitalize an ailing business. How to turbo charge your products and services to generate higher and higher profits. a remarkable system of making what you do a "household" name.

Cat No 004 CD

31 Laws of Money
Dr. Abib Olamitoye

How the understanding of the Laws of Money can grant a solid foundation of prosperity.

Cat No 005 CD

**KAIZEN
The Good Change**
Dr. Abib Olamitoye

How do you eat an Elephant? One bite at a time. The baby step approach to incremental improvement using the classical suggestion scheme. A fresh approach to innovation through relentless pursuit of excellence.

Cat No 006 CD

How To Sell Well
Dr. Abib Olamitoye

Why people agree to buy things and how you can tailor your sales effort in order to sell more.

Cat No 007 CD

The "win win" solution to negotiation.

Cat No 008 CD

How to remove incompetent employee without discord. They walk away and still remain friends while you create vacancies for competent wealth creators that add value.

Cat No 009 CD

How to conduct a successful meeting and generate the greatest and finest ideas from meeting participants.

Cat No 010 CD

How to stay stubbornly committed to success in the face of adversity. The inspiration to keep on keeping on.

Cat No 011 CD

How to work less while earning more.

Cat No 012 CD

How to make people do what you want.

Cat No 013 CD

The first Law of Management is to hire the right people. Here is the finest approach to hiring competent and dedicated employees.

Cat No 014 CD

How to work on priority tasks; organize your life for effectiveness and resourcefulness; balance work and leisure, run a stress free and productive day.

Cat No 015 CD

A workshop on goal setting: How to program the brain for success. Almost effortlessly, you sit, imagine, feel, write and end up with irresistible and compelling purpose, vision and direction for your life.

Cat No 016 CD

The backbone of successful business management. How you can orchestrate a fine and enduring architecture for a sustainable business enterprise.

Cat No 017 CD

The stress free way to handle life and business.

Cat No 018 CD

The simple steps to sharing responsibility and authority in the work place. How to involve people, commit people and empower people.

Cat No 019 CD

Magical steps to healing, excellent health and vigorous energy.

ENQUIRIES
htenacademy@aol.com
villageboy2009@ymail.com